FIRST, WE MUST LISTEN

Living in a Multicultural Society

Friendship Press
New York

Copyright © 1996 Friendship Press

Editorial Offices: 475 Riverside Drive, New York, NY 10115
Distribution Offices: PO Box 37844, Cincinnati, OH 45222-0844

Layout and design by Patricia Kellis.

Manufactured in the United States of America.

Library of Congress Cataloging—in—Publication Date

First, we must listen : living in a multicultural society / [edited by] Anne Leo Ellis
      p. cm.
      ISBN 0-377-00302-6
      1. United States—Ethnic relations. 2. Canada—Ethnic relations. 3. Ethnic
relations—Religious aspects—Christianity. 4. Pluralism (Social sciences)—United
States. 5. Pluralism (Social sciences)—Canada. 6. Sociology, Christian—United
States. 7. Sociology, Christian—Canada. I. Ellis, Anne Leo.
E184.A1F575 1996
305.8'00973—dc20   95-53704
                                                                        CIP

CONTENTS

Acknowledgments 5

Introduction 7

One: Six Personal Reflections 9
   Kim Uyede-Kai 10
   Ada Maríe Isasi-Díaz 14
   Stan McKay 19
   Donald Ng 24
   Traci West 27
   Peggy McIntosh 29

Two: Reexamining the Past: How Did We Get Here? 35
   George Tinker 36
   Katie Geneva Cannon 43
   Richard Rodriguez 51
   Mary Swander 55
   Kim Uyede-Kai 63

Three: Assessing the Future: A Multicultural North America .. 65
   James A. Banks 66
   Demographic Studies 70
   William H. Frey and Jonathan Tilove 74
   Cornel West 76
   George Tinker 81
   Richard Rodriguez 83

Four: A Biblical Vision: From Diversity to Pluralism 87
   Daniel F. Romero 88

Five: Barriers Among Us and Within Ourselves 91
   Anne Bathurst Gilson and Barbara A. Weaver 92

Six: Striving Toward a Multicultural Society 101
   First Church, Hartford, Connecticut 102
   First Baptist Church, Los Angeles, California 107
   Ruth S. Morales 109
   Oakhurst Presbyterian Church, Decatur, Georgia ... 111
   Inez Fleming 112
   David Ng 114
   Joyce Carlson 120

Postscript 125

ACKNOWLEDGMENTS

We are grateful to several publishers and authors for permission to reprint from their published works as follows:

Part One

Uyede-Kai: Used by permission artemis enterprises; excerpt from *Gathered by the River: Reflections and Essays of Women Doing Ministry* (Gertrude Lebans, ed.) RR#2, Box 54, Dundas, ON Canada L9H 5E2.

Isasi-Díaz: From *Inheriting Our Mothers' Gardens* edited by Letty M. Russell, Kwok Pui-Lan, Ada María Isasi-Díaz, and Katie Geneva Cannon. © 1988 Letty M. Russell. Used by permission of Westminster John Knox Press. All Rights Reserved.

McKay: Used by permission of The United Church Publishing House: *Journey from Fisher River* by Joyce Carlson, selected passages from pages 32 to 80.

Ng: "Portrait of Asian American Youth," by Donald Ng in *The Ongoing Journey: Awakening the Spiritual Life in At-Risk Youth* by Robert Coles, et al. (The Boys Town Press, 1995). Reprinted with permission of the publisher.

West: "I am NOT Your Diversity," by Traci West. Reprinted with permission from *The Other Side*, 300 W. Apsley, Philadelphia, PA 19144 (215-849-2178). New subscriptions $19.97 per year.

McIntosh: © Peggy McIntosh 1988. Permission to duplicate must be obtained from the author at Wellesley College Center for Research on Women, Wellesley, MA 02181 (617) 283–2520.

Part Two

Tinker: Excerpts from chapter 6. Reprinted by permission from *Missionary Conquest: The Gospel and Native American Cultural Genocide* by George Tinker; copyright © 1993 Augsburg Fortress.

Cannon: From *Inheriting Our Mothers' Gardens* edited by Letty M. Russell, Kwok Pui-Lan, Ada María Isasi-Díaz, and Katie Geneva Cannon. © 1988 Letty M. Russell. Used by permission of Westminster John Knox Press. All Rights Reserved.

Rodriguez: From *Hunger of Memory* by Richard Rodriguez. Reprinted by permission of David R. Godine, Publisher, Inc. Copyright © 1982 by Richard Rodriguez.

Swander: From OUT OF THIS WORLD by Mary Swander. Copyright © 1995 by Mary Swander. Used by permission of Viking Penguin, a division of Penguin Books USA Inc.

Uyede-Kai: © Kim Uyede-Kai 1995. Reprinted from *Fire From the Ashes: Reflections on Lighting the Shadows* © 1995, The United Church of Canada, Etobicoke, Canada. Reprinted by permission.

Part Three

Banks: From an essay "Multicultural Education: For Freedom's Sake" by James Banks. Reprinted from *Educational Leadership* (December 1991/January 1992). Used by permission of the author.

U.S. Demographics: The tables are from Desk Reference Series No. 1, "American Diversity." Source: *American Demographics* magazine, © 1991. Reprinted with permission.

Frey and Tilove: "Immigrants In, Native Whites Out," by William H. Frey and Jonathan Tilove. *New York Times Magazine* 20 August 1995. Copyright © 1995 by The New York Times Company. Reprinted by permission.

West: Excerpts from Introduction in *Race Matters,* by Cornel West (Beacon Press, 1993). From RACE MATTERS by Cornel West. Copyright © 1993 by Cornel West. Reprinted by permission of Beacon Press.

Tinker: Excerpts from chapter 2. Reprinted by permission from *Missionary Conquest: The Gospel and Native American Cultural Genocide* by George Tinker; copyright © 1993 Augsburg Fortress.

Rodriguez: Courtesy of Pacific News Service, San Francisco, California (11 Sept. 1995). Used by permission.

Part Four

Romero: Excerpts from the chapter "Biblical and Theological Insights" from *Our Futures Inextricably Linked: A Vision of Pluralism* by Daniel F. Romero (Cleveland: UCBHM, 1994). Reprinted with permission of the Pilgrim Press, Cleveland, Ohio.

Part Six

Fleming: Copyright © by Nibs Stroupe and Inez Fleming. Excerpts from *While We Run This Race: Confronting the Power of Racism in a Southern Church,* by Nibs Stroupe and Inez Fleming (Orbis Books, 1995) is reprinted with permission of the publisher.

Ng: "Sojourners Bearing Gifts: Pacific Asian American Christian Education" by David Ng in *Ethnicity in the Education of the Church* (June 1987) is reprinted with permission of the editor Charles R. Foster.

INTRODUCTION

The premise of this book, persuasively borne out by demographic studies and scholarly research, is that we in Canada and the United States are, four years before the millennium, a multicultural society, and that this trend will continue during the coming decades—on both the secular and religious fronts. Furthermore, unlike the past, we will not be overwhelmingly of European ancestry. This is a reality that European Americans—currently still the majority culture in the United States and Canada—need to grasp. It is equally important to recognize that in the United States, the predominantly African American—European American debate has expanded significantly to include Hispanics, Asians, Pacific Islanders, and Native Americans as part of American reality and culture. (Indeed, demographic studies suggest that Hispanic Americans will soon overtake African Americans as the largest minority group in the United States.)

The debate does not stop there. For within each of these groups there are further national/tribal/ethnic allegiances. How all of us as residents of a Canada and a United States representing many cultures deal with such issues will determine the shape of our religious and secular lives, and of our societies in the twenty-first century.

Many persons from a variety of ethnic and racial groups in the United States and Canada have important ideas and strong opinions about these issues. They can share experiences that seared and shaped their lives, and helped them formulate their own philosophies. Within the church, many have found that life with others in the Gospel has not been without the pain, exclusion, confusion, and conflict engendered by racial and ethnic misunderstanding and suspicion. Some in the majority culture—but far too few—have learned that their unacknowledged or unrecognized privileges are real, often at the expense of their sisters and brothers in Christ, albeit sisters and brothers of another race or culture. These few have struggled to change their own racist perceptions and to help others change theirs.

It is our hope that the components of this book: articles, conversations, vignettes and graphs, reflecting the lives and stating frank opinions of persons from many ethnic and racial groups, will lead to constructive debate, analysis, and prayer, as we—all of us representing these races and cultures—seek to find avenues for living together as God's people in Canada and the United States in the coming century.

The book is divided into six parts. Though each part is designed as the basis of one group session to be used with an accompanying study guide and video, it—or the book as a whole—can also stand alone, to be read without further discussion or interaction. Either way, it is our hope that you will find this collection useful in the search for a more profound understanding of matters crucial to all our lives as Christians and as citizens in a multicultural North America.

First, we must listen. Carefully, thoughtfully, without interruption, without hidden agendas, without preconceptions. Next, we need to think. And talk. With each other. As openly as possible, prepared for misunderstanding and anger, but also for healing, comprehension, reconciliation—friendship. Such are the currents we seek to stimulate. If these essays and interviews, these personal reflections, these analyses and deconstructions of historical memory start or continue thoughtful conversation, self-analysis, and prayer, they will have served an important purpose.

Part One
SIX PERSONAL REFLECTIONS

We begin our study with five first-person accounts by women and men representing a variety of cultures who share with us personal experiences and observations about life in a multicultural society still overwhelmingly of European ancestry. Highly successful in their chosen endeavors, all struggling to be true to their heritages in a society dominated by European culture, they explore, in a variety of ways, what this means—what it's like.

Kim Uyede-Kai, Japanese-Canadian; Ada María Isasi-Díaz, Cuban-American; Stan McKay, Aboriginal Canadian; Donald Ng, Chinese-American; and Traci West, African American, approach their material in very different ways, but one thing comes through in each: the sense that they, as members of ethnic or racial groups not of the majority culture, have been excluded and marginalized, and that few European Americans/Canadians understand what this really means in daily life and work; that it is a struggle requiring immense courage, tenacity, dignity, and sense of self. Some of the authors speak gently; others express anger and frustration. The final essay, in order to provide a tool for serious and ongoing self-examination by members of the dominant European American culture, is by Peggy McIntosh, a European American academic. It is important to note that each of these authors speaks as an individual observer and thinker, not as a representative of her or his particular racial or ethnic group.

Kim Uyede-Kai

As a third-generation Japanese-Canadian, Kim Uyede-Kai asks why someone like herself is still perceived as an immigrant because of Asian features. And why is she still frequently the single person of other than European ancestry in church leadership situations? The following piece appeared in the book **Gathered by the River: Reflections and Essays of Women Doing Ministry.** *Ms. Uyede Kai, a member of the Ethnic Ministries Council of the United Church of Canada, is working toward a Master of Divinity at Emmanuel College, Toronto, Canada.*

My favourite fabric is the Japanese *furoshiki*, a large square of textured cloth on which is woven a brightly coloured floral and bamboo pattern. The many coloured threads are patterned to give a distinctly Japanese appearance. As a sort of Japanese version of a shopping bag, it is used to wrap and transport such things as a potluck dish and can be tied around something as unexpected as a pan of lasagna. This Japanese-looking weaving with its sometimes seemingly incongruous contents is, in many ways, very much an image of who I am.

Immigrated genes don't change much, so I have the same racial features as my Japanese ancestors even after three and four generations on Canadian soil. I'm regularly mistaken for an immigrant. The same law does not hold for a transported culture. I have been influenced as much by the nineteenth-century Japanese culture of my ancestors as the Japanese Canadian culture and experiences of my parents and family, and the western culture of the Canadian urban schools, church and society in which I grew up and live out my life. The threads of these genetic and cultural elements make for an ongoing, complex weaving of cultural diversity containing a few surprises.

My Grandfather Maruya was born in Canada to Japanese immigrants. He was as fluent in English as he was in Japanese, which he spoke with a Canadian accent. Because he shared a home with us and spoke English, he was a strong influence in my life. As a young child, I often tagged along when he visited his Italian-speaking friends. He was always welcome because he had learned enough Italian to be able to converse with his co-workers and neighbours and had picked up quite a bit of their culture. So, although English was the first language I learned, Italian was, strangely enough, the second language I remember hearing. The cultural cross-over also lingers because, to this day, I still must have Pannetone bread at Christmas.

The community, church and schools I grew up in were almost all Caucasian of Italian, Ukrainian, Dutch, Anglo and Quebecois heritages, with the exception of a few multi-generation Black Canadian, Chinese and Japanese families. It was the only environment I knew, so I never questioned it and was comfortable enough. My experiences with the Japanese Canadian community had been strictly limited to gatherings with family, family friends and an annual community picnic. Like many others, I believed racial minorities had "made it" when they were able to fully integrate by blending in, identifying with and being accepted by the Caucasian majority.

I came to a Japanese Canadian United Church at nineteen years and was shocked to find myself breathing a suppressed sigh of (cultural) relief. A black hair lying accusingly on a table was no longer necessarily mine. I would no longer be type cast to play the part of the foreign immigrant in a church school play. I could hear affirming references to Japanese Canadian cultural and war experiences in worship and in casual conversation. After years of hearing the Anglo and Scottish experiences raised up almost exclusively, I began to realize that part of me also needed the authentic affirmation of my Japanese Canadian experience. I had been racially visible, but my culture and experiences had been invisible.

I went from a Caucasian majority environment in which I was perceived to be quiet, passive, inhibited, ineffective, to a Japanese Canadian majority environment in which I was perceived to be radical, aggressive, disagreeable and disrespectful. In some ways, it was very freeing, because that part of me is not fully recognized in many Caucasian contexts because my personality and style do not fit the standard mold. Same person, same personality, different rules.

Still, it was quite a culture shock to see the rules espoused by my parents and their families lived out in an entire church community. I wasn't prepared for the land mine of cultural norms and standards, some of which I was totally unfamiliar with and others of which I had rebelled against as a youth. The Japanese Canadian rules of holding back, not imposing, maintaining the family honour, returning favour for favour, duty and obligation, all proliferated in binding abundance. I'm sure I stepped on a lot of toes while I tried to decipher the unwritten codes of behavior and thinking, and determined which I could accept and which to modify or reject.

The process, however, was a rich learning experience. The more anecdotal stories I heard, the better I was able to understand where the rules of behaviour came from and how those rules ensured their survival during World War II. I heard what it was like to grow up Japanese in British Columbia, to have homes, businesses and possessions taken away and sold for next to nothing, to be herded into internment camps and branded "enemy aliens", to be forced to move east to find places to live and work in still racist communities. "Integration" was enforced and encouraged wherever they settled and worshiped. In order to get on with their lives, Japanese Canadians kept a low profile, worked very hard and did their best to integrate into the Caucasian majority society. Many did eventually form Japanese membership churches for their own language and worship needs, but many also joined local churches.

Japanese race and culture are not thought to be the same issues as they were forty or even twenty years ago. People now tell me that they are colour blind, that they no longer notice that I don't look like them. They think of me as "one of them" because I speak their language and can blend in. When I was growing up, that would have been the ultimate compliment. I yearned to look like and be treated like a Caucasian so that my racial differences would not be centered out. My Japanese features were a constant source of shame and embarrassment to me. I was teased in the playground because of the shape of my eyes, chastised by teachers because my parents didn't teach me the Japanese language (even more shameful that they knew too little to teach), taught that Japanese features were not beautiful or handsome unless they looked Caucasian, never remembered because "all Orientals look alike." It was a slow process to unpack those burdens of painful racial discrimination and to recognize the pain for what it was.

I began to see that for a racial minority not to be noticed in a Caucasian majority meant not acceptance, but meant invisibility, being patronized, buying into the belief that the Caucasian standard of beauty was the ultimate in desired looks, that the Western cultures were superior and Eastern cultures were foreign and inferior. Integrating meant adopting and valuing the dominant culture and traditions, and devaluing and dismissing ancestral culture and traditions. Although Asian food is much more common than it once was, I find it sad that many of my sons' Asian immigrant school friends are still too embarrassed to bring "ethnic" food for lunch and insist their parents pack plain sandwiches.

Membership in an ethnic church also taught me how the wider church sees ethnic-specific congregations. When people say that I am from "one of our ethnic churches," I feel a figurative pat on the head. Being small in stature and size and looking younger than my years, I am used to being treated like a child, but it was a new experience for me to hear an entire group of congregations being patronized. Missionaries did some wonderful work in the past among racial minority groups and particularly among Japanese Canadians, but the mentality from the colonialization days of the past still lingers. It is difficult to change the well-meaning "doing for, doing to" attitudes of mission into "being with" because they are so intangible and deeply rooted. Caucasian persons with some experience in non-white countries and ethnic church settings still ask, "What can we do for you?" Ethnic churches are rarely valued as congregations on equal footing as the rest of the church because they are still seen as a foreign language stepping stone that minorities leave once they feel comfortable enough in English to join a local majority church.

Racism takes many forms in the church and is an issue I am constantly faced with. Whenever I speak about systemic racism experienced by Japanese Canadians, someone always draws parallels to the United Empire Loyalists and, more recently, the Irish in Canada. For some reason, it is difficult for some people to see that racial discrimination based on Asian features continues today in a way that is not experienced by Irish Canadians. Backlash against any new wave of Asian immigration is always felt by all Asians, regardless of countries of origin or number of years in Canada. So, whether the experiences of racism are different or whether they are the same, it does not change the fact that racism exists. Blatant or violent acts against any one race are fairly easy to identify, but subtle or systemic racial discrimination is more difficult to get a handle on and address.

When I received an invitation to attend a United Church leadership development event looking toward the twenty-first century, I was excited to be given an opportunity to reflect on my experiences in the church, to learn new skills, to creatively integrate body, mind and spirit in the company of people I knew and those I might come to know. I had met and valued many people in my work on several church committees, many with a particular focus on ethnic ministries, and looked forward to sharing this learning experience with at least some of them. I went—open to being energized, affirmed in my lay ministry, excited by new visions. It did indeed turn out to be a life-giving event. But there were also some uncomfortable learnings that reminded me that what I look like continues to give name to my struggles and causes some people and systems to set me apart.

An incident at the first meal reminded me of the reality of my racial features. My table of strangers was sharing general information about ourselves. When I asked the woman across the table where she was from, it became clear that she couldn't hear me even as I asked again and the person sitting next to her repeated my question. I thought I had spoken too quickly or too quietly but then found it strange that someone sitting even farther away had heard me. The expression on the woman's face remained with me for some reason, and later it occurred to me that she did not look as though she had not heard me but rather that she had not understood my words. I'd seen that look before and, although there are some who will say I was too sensitive, it was the look of someone who had trouble subconsciously reconciling my Japanese face with my Canadian-accented English. This was a piece of the reality of being a racial minority woman in the church.

Later that same evening, I looked around the large circle of almost 60 faces and became increasingly aware that I was the only one who was not Caucasian. None of the racial-minority women and men I knew to be in church leadership were present. Having attended many similar racially represented gatherings, this was not an unusual or uncomfortable circumstance for me to find myself in. But the implications of this "hand-picked," almost all-Caucasian church leadership event became increasingly distressing to me as the weekend progressed and in the months that followed. What did it mean that so few participants noticed the racial exclusiveness of a major leadership event? What did it mean that the capabilities and gifts of racial minorities in leadership were not considered for inclusion in the church of the future? What did it mean that while most racial minorities consider themselves to be very much a part of the whole church, they are absent from almost all recognized leadership positions beyond the local church? And what did it mean for me to have to raise these questions on my own because there was no one else to do it with me?

It is a strange paradox that racial minorities can be so visible and present and yet be so invisible and absent. Yet many people, racial minorities included, say with conviction that racial minorities are very much a part of the whole church and there are no limits as to where they could go. But, for whatever reason, the glass ceiling that is evident in the corporate world also applies to the church. The United Church of Canada elected the Very Rev. Dr. Sang Chul Lee as its Moderator, but the upper-level management of its General Council Offices remains Caucasian as do the majority of its committees, World Outreach being an exception. Racial minorities are not present, and they are not there to know that they are absent. In looking at themselves, the churches are beginning to say that they are not racially representative of Canadian society in their leadership and are wondering how to change that.

Racial minorities are beginning to wonder as well. Absence goes much deeper than not being invited. As I began to question what it means for me to be a racial minority woman in my context, I also began to ask questions about my theological context in the United Church. Feminist theology has great relevance for me but is done from Caucasian women's experience. Asian feminist theology, especially by Korean theologian Chung Hyun Kyung, touches a nerve but still is not the Asian Canadian experience. I deeply appreciate what our First Nations people share about their spirituality and wonder how the honouring of the earth was part of my farming and fishing ancestors' spirituality. I attend wonderful workshops on body movement with a Hebrew focus and wonder how I could get in touch with the Japanese response to body and spirit that comes from my ancestors' Buddhist roots. Indeed, I wonder what parts of Buddhist spirituality I carry in my Japanese Canadian culture and what it can say to my Christianity.

I have been blessed with opportunities to explore these questions with other racial minority women and men in ministry. Because we are few in number and isolated by distance and busy lives, I appreciate the support these gatherings bring. It is not always easy to be alone. My life is far richer for the majority church women's gatherings and networks I have been and still need to be part of, but the coming together of racial-minority women is particularly special. Although I find myself a minority among the minority because I don't have the immigrant experience that most of them do, we share similar experiences and struggles of marginalization and sexism in the Caucasian majority church and society, as well as within our race-specific churches and communities.

Each thread connecting my new experiences, new learnings and reflections weaves its way into existing threads that take on a new pattern, reflecting the integration that is so much a part of my psyche. To do it with integrity and in community is the challenge. As my Japanese looks and cultural experiences continue to shape my ministry in a Caucasian majority church, it becomes apparent that the weaving of my *furoshiki* goes on, with colour and texture, with new and interesting things yet to be unfolded.

Ada María Isasi-Díaz

Ada María Isasi-Díaz writes about the trauma of her dual Cuban and American allegiances and makes a powerful statement about the struggles of a Hispanic-American feminist. Her essay appears in the book Inheriting Our Mothers' Gardens: Feminist Theology in Third World Perspective. *Dr. Isasi-Díaz is Associate Professor of Ethics and Theology at Drew University, Madison, New Jersey.*

After twenty-six years of being away from my mother's garden, I returned to Cuba for a visit in January 1987. For two very special weeks, with the greatest of intentionality, I walked around *la tierra que me vio nacer* (the land that witnessed my birth), the land I have missed so very much. I tried to notice everything around me. My senses were constantly on alert, trying to imbibe every single detail, trying to sear into my heart the sights, sounds, smells of that beautiful island from which I have been gone for over half my life. The beauty of its majestic palm trees, the striking combination of green fields and white sand, the calm blue waters of the tropical sea, the immense variety of the colorful tropical plants and flowers, the exciting rhythms of its music, my Cuban sisters and brothers—no wonder Columbus said, when he landed there in 1492, "This is the most beautiful land human eyes have ever seen."

Every minute of the two weeks I was in Cuba I reminded myself I was only visiting; I was going to have to leave in a very short time. There I felt the same as I feel in the United States: a foreigner. I am caught between two worlds, neither of which is fully mine, both of which are partially mine. I do not belong in the Cuba of today; I do not belong in the States. I am repeating the history of my mother and of her mother. Grandma came to Cuba as a young woman in search of a brother who had left their home in the small village of Tineo in northern Spain and had never even written to his family. Once in Cuba, she was never to go back to her native land. My mother was forty-eight when we came to live in the United States because of the political situation in Cuba. She has never gone back and now, at the age of seventy-three, has little hope of seeing Cuba again.

As a foreigner in an alien land, I have not inherited a garden from my mother but rather a bunch of cuttings. Beautiful but rootless flowering plants—that is my inheritance Rooting and replanting them requires extra work on the part of the gardener; it requires much believing in myself to make my life flourish away from the tropical sun of Cuba. Some of the flowers I have inherited from my mother help me to deal with this situation; others at times can hinder me.

One of my ongoing gardening tasks is to find a place to plant the flowers I have inherited from my mother. At the age of eighteen I was uprooted from my country. What I thought would be a hiatus turned into twenty-six years. I am beginning to suspect it might well become the rest of my life. For many different reasons I have had no choice but to try to plant my garden in the United States. But belonging to the culture of one of the "minority groups" has meant that the plants in my garden have been seen as weeds or exotica; they are either plucked up or treated as a rarity. In general they are not accepted as part of the common garden of the dominant U.S. culture.

Most people think I should not find it too difficult to adapt my flowers and my gardening style—my cultural inheritance—to a new situation. After all, culture is always changing; it is dynamic. The fact is, however, that by belonging to a minority culture within another culture, the changing dynamic of my culture becomes a nonorganic force. The changes taking place in the Hispanic culture in the United States do not start from within but are imposed from without. These inorganic changes do not enhance the culture but rather negate it. Forced changes bring not flourishing but wilting and dying. A culture forced to change by outside forces suffers violence; its values begin to deteriorate. A culture that is not valued, whether by being ignored or by being commercially exploited, is in danger of losing little by little its will to live.[1]

This is what happens to Hispanic culture in the United States. It is sacked and raped every time we are told that our children cannot learn in Spanish in school, when our customs are ridiculed, when our cultural artifacts—typical dress, music, etc.—are commercialized. The intergenerational crisis among Hispanics goes beyond the usual differences between youth and older people. This crisis is directly connected to the lack of importance and significance given to Hispanic culture by the dominant culture. On top of the identity crisis that all young people suffer as they search for their own worth and a way to be themselves, Hispanic youths suffer from the violence against our culture in this society.

No wonder they try to hide their *abuelitas*, anglicize their names, and join the world of drugs in order to have the money they think will bring recognition. No wonder I have never been able to plant my garden successfully in this society.

Trying to Plant My Garden

In the 1960s I tried to plant my garden in the convent. The enormous value given to family and community in my culture seemed to me to be the very core of this style of life. But, at least in the time when I was there, the restrictions on personal relationships that were part of life in the convent made true community life impossible. The emotional intensity of my Cuban culture was also out of place in the convent. The very poor and oppressed of Peru, among whom I worked for three years, taught me *too much*, and I could not maintain a lifestyle in which people talked about poverty while living a privileged life. Finally, my unwillingness to repress my spontaneity and passion led me to realize that my garden could not flourish within the convent walls.

If not in the convent, as a Roman Catholic woman, where could I make bloom the flower of my commitment to the poor and the oppressed? The search led me to the feminist movement. I was born a feminist on Thanksgiving weekend, 1975, when over one thousand Roman Catholic women met to insist on the right of women to be ordained to a renewed priestly ministry in our church. Failing, as the overwhelming majority of humans do, to remember my bodily birth, I am privileged to remember every detail of this birth to the struggle for liberation. But the process of "giving birth to myself"[2] was not an all-of-a-sudden experience; in many ways the process had started years before.

I spent the early part of my life in Cuba, where I belonged to the dominant race and the middle class. Growing up in the 1950s, I did not notice the oppressive structures of sexism operative in my country. But I was always attracted to struggling along with those "who had less than I did"—as I thought of the oppressed then. As a matter of fact, it was precisely that attraction which made me come to understand my vocation to the ministry. It was that attraction which I now understand as the seed of my commitment to the struggle for liberation.

At age eighteen I entered the convent, a protected way of life that used to carry with it much prestige and privilege. Therefore, the few times I came into contact with the broader society during the first eight years of my adulthood, I was treated with deference, respect, and even reverence. My life within the convent walls was very difficult, and at the time I did not have the lenses needed to understand ethnic prejudice. I was greatly misunderstood and suffered much because of it, but I did not have a good analysis of what was happening to me and how I was being treated by the other nuns.

By 1975, therefore, the only oppression I was aware of was the one I suffer within the church simply because I am a woman. It is no surprise, then, that it was in relation to church teaching and practice that I came to understand the dynamics of oppression and joined the struggle for liberation. The 1975 Women's Ordination Conference was such an intense experience that when I emerged from the hotel where we had held the three-day conference, I realized I was perceiving the world in a different way. It took a few months before I realized what the difference was that I was seeing. My eyes had been opened to the reality of sexism. My whole life had been affected; how I saw myself and what I was to do with my life had changed radically.

The struggle against sexism in the Roman Catholic Church has been the school where I have learned about feminism, as well as the main arena in which I have carried out my struggle for liberation during the last twelve years. I rejoice in the sisterhood in whose creation I have participated and am grateful for all that I have learned from the women involved in the Womanchurch movement. This became my home. Soon I proceeded to plant my own garden there; however, that brought conflict into the sisterhood. As long as I toiled in the garden of Anglo feminism, I was welcomed. But as I started to claim a space in the garden to plant my own flowers, the ethnic/racist prejudice prevalent in society reared its head within the Womanchurch movement.

The issue was and is power.[3] Somewhat naively I had thought that together we would decide not only how to garden but what the garden was to look like, what it would be. But the Anglo feminists, being part of the dominant culture, deal with Hispanic women—and other racial/ethnic women—differently from the way they deal with each other. They take for granted that feminism in the United States is *their* garden, and therefore they will decide what manner of work racial/ethnic women will do there.

By the time I began to experience all this, I had learned much about the dynamics of oppression and prejudice and I could understand what was going on. However, what took me totally by surprise was the inability or unwillingness of the Anglo feminists to acknowledge their prejudice. Most feminists "believe that because they are feminists, they cannot be racists." Anglo feminists, like all liberals, sooner or later, have come to the point at which they are willing to "acknowledge that racism exists, reluctantly of course, but nobody admits to being a racist."[4] While whitewashing their personal sins of racism/ethnic prejudice—pun intended—in the restful waters of guilt, they continue to control access to power within the movement. Anglo feminists need to understand that as long as they refuse to recognize that power-over is an intrinsic element of their racism/ethnic prejudice, they will continue to do violence to feminism. As a liberative praxis, feminism has to do with radically changing the patriarchal understandings of power, which are operative even in the feminist movement. Anglo feminists need to remember that, in order to undo patriarchy, we must create societies in which people can be self-defining and self-determining. To achieve that, power has to be transformed and shared.

True sharing of power leads to mutuality, and that is what we Hispanic feminists ask of Anglo feminists. It is not a matter of their allowing us to share in what they define as good. Nor is it only a matter of each one of us respecting what the other says and defending her right to say it. Mutuality asks us to give serious consideration to what the other is saying, not only to respect it but to be willing to accept it as good for all. Hispanic feminists' understandings must be included in what is normative for all feminists. Our priorities must be considered to be just as important as the priorities of the Anglo feminists. All feminists must work together on deciding the priorities for the movement. This is the only thing that will allow me to continue to believe that the feminist movement "is one of the few parties left in town where we can all come together for the larger common cause. But if we're really going to boogie, power has to be shared."[5]

One of the easiest ways to understand the structure of power in society and within the feminist movement is to look at how we both construct and express what we think. Let us, therefore, look at language. For example, the fact that the word "women" refers only to middle- and upper-strata white women shows who decides what is normative. All the rest of us, in order not to be totally invisible, have to add adjectives to the word: *poor* women, *Black* women, *Hispanic* women. *Poor* women means white, underemployed, or unemployed women. *Black* women means poor Black women; Black women who are not poor are called *educated* Black women. Women *of color* in reality refers only to Black women, with the rest of us racial/ethnic women being added on as an afterthought—if we are given any thought at all. *Salvadoran* women, *Guatemalan* women—at present they command the attention of our liberal communities. After all, what we need to help change are their countries, not the United States! *Hispanic* women refers to poor women, usually Puerto Ricans, Dominicans, Mexicans, and Mexican Americans. Then there are *Cuban* women—those middle-and upper-class women down there in Miami who vote conservative. Since heterosexuality is normative in society, that meaning is also included in the words "feminists" or "women." The "others" have to be qualified: *lesbian* women, *bisexual* women.

As these examples show, power always rests with those who define the norm. Language offers us a very important tool for understanding the power dynamics in society and in the feminist movement. It clearly points out to me, at least, where I will not be able to plant my own garden and in which gardens I will never be anything but a hired hand at the very best. The net result of all this, I believe, is an impoverishment of the feminist movement, which in turn arrests its effectiveness and contribution as a liberation movement. As long as Anglo feminists do not share power within the movement with Hispanic, Black, and other racial/ethnic women, the movement will only be capable of bringing about a liberalization of those who control and oppress. Under these circumstances, the feminist movement might moderate patriarchy but it will not do away with it.

As a Hispanic I belong to a marginalized group in this society and have had to struggle to understand and deal with the siege mentality we suffer. The need to protect ourselves against discrimination is such an integral part of our lives that we are unable or unwilling to critique ourselves. It is difficult to see criticism as constructive when we are not valued by society. Those of us who as feminists criticize sexism in the Hispanic culture are often belittled and accused of selling out to the Anglo women. But Anglo feminists call into question our integrity and praxis as Hispanic feminists when we are not willing to criticize Hispanic men and culture in public. I would like to suggest that this kind of horizontal violence is linked to both internalized oppression and the siege mentality.

The challenge that lies before me has many different facets. I must struggle to convince myself and other Hispanics that our goal has to be liberation and not participation in oppressive situations and societies. We must not give in to internalized oppression and a siege mentality. We must be willing to look at ourselves and examine our experiences in view of our liberation and continue to insist, no matter where we are, on being

Endnotes

1. My understandings of culture are greatly influenced by Geertz and Scannone. See Clifford Geertz, *The Interpretations of Culture* (New York: Basic Books, 1973), and Juan Carlos Scannone, "Teología, Cultura Popular y Discernimiento," in *Cultura Popular y Filosofía de la Liberación* (Buenos Aires: Fernando García Cambeiro, 1975), pp. 241–270.
2. As I type in my apartment I face a poster that reads, I AM A WOMAN GIVING BIRTH TO MYSELF.
3. *Building Feminist Theory: Essays from QUEST* (Harlow, Essex: Longman Group, 1981).
4. Marcia Ann Gillespie, "My Gloves Are Off, Sisters," *MS Magazine*, April 1987, pp. 19–20.
5. Ibid.
6. Three books that have been very important for me in the area of friendship are Margaret Farley, *Personal*

included in setting the norm of the feminist movement. Then I have to find renewed strength and commitment to struggle with Anglo feminists over the issue of sharing power with all feminists, unless their goal is to replace one oppressor with another. Finally, I have to challenge myself and others to understand that, as feminists, the changes we are advocating will change the world radically and that we need to begin to live out those changes so they can become a reality.[7] The only way we can move ahead is by living the reality we envision. Our preferred future as feminists will only flower if we allow it to be firmly rooted in us and among us. It is up to us to change our lives radically if we want our world to change.

Commitments (New York: Harper & Row, 1986); Isabel C. Heyward, The Redemption of God (Lanham, Md.: University Press of America, 1982); and Janice Raymond, A Passion for Friends (Boston: Beacon Press, 1986).
7. See Sonia Johnson, Going Out of Our Minds: The Metaphysics of Liberation (Freedom, Calif.: Crossing Press, 1987).

Stan McKay

Stan McKay describes his sense of conflict and alienation as a young Aboriginal-Canadian student within systems of education that were foreign and often hostile. He speaks about his Cree and Ojibway roots, and his need for a Christian faith that has room for his own understanding of spirituality. These selections come from Journey from Fisher River: A Celebration of the Spirituality of a People through the Life of Stan McKay, *by Joyce Carlson. The Reverend Stan McKay is director of the Dr. Jessie Saulteaux Resource Centre near Winnepeg, Manitoba, and a former Moderator of the United Church of Canada.*

There wasn't really anything there with any meaning. I went to school with my sister Emily, who was two years older. We did have a place to go back to, a family that cared about us, a community that had some health. We had a sense of home. We could look forward to that. On occasion we would get letters, although they would have been opened and read before we got them. Our contact with family and community came in that way. This was important because much of what happened didn't have any connection to life and hope. Others didn't have that connection.

We were in an interesting location up above the town of Birtle. I'd look out over the town in the evening; all the lights would be on. I knew that there was a life, a community down there to which I did not belong. I spent time with the other students, but there were few opportunities to discuss things important to me.

At school, we were told when to get up, when to go to bed, when to eat. We lived through those days and went to classes that lacked creative teaching. We were going to someone else's school. Why would you learn the chemical formulas of all the elements of the earth?, I wondered. Why would you do that in preparation for life on a reservation? On the reserve, one learned the names of things one needed and would be involved with. But why would you memorize columns of information on atomic weights and formulas for chemical change?

It was all abstract. I didn't find that kind of learning easy. I didn't have a background, an understanding, of scientific ideas. They didn't have connection with my reality. It was then I began to realize that I hadn't read much. I came to the study of English out of my reservation experience. The teacher expected me to read English novels and understand them and the culture in which they had been written. It was a very strange culture to understand. To be able to assess and write about it in ways that the teacher wanted was not easy.

The other students and I had different advantages and disadvantages than most of the people in the high school. This made it almost impossible for 90 per cent of us to make it through the system. The learning offered was culturally inappropriate. There was no understanding of this among the teachers at that time. The education system had been a problem for many years. Aboriginal language and cultural values were denied, especially our respect for humility.

For example, in our culture you wouldn't look into the eyes of someone you respected. You would talk quietly and keep your head down because that was a sign of respect in the Aboriginal community. So, the aggression and competitiveness that the school encouraged was against our cultural values. I was encouraged to be smarter than others. This went against everything I had learned in my home and family, where I had been taught to help and accept others. It went against the cultural values of my village.

Individualism and aggressiveness continue to be the hardest things for me to deal with in any kind of educational setting where people strive to be first. One is forced to deny friends. Aboriginal society has a lot of trouble with that. Aboriginal people don't learn academically, nor by trying to deal with abstract ideas; rather, our history has been one of learning by observation. Everyone learns; everyone is a trapper. You don't receive a pass or fail on the trapline. Everyone has a place and everyone can learn, maybe in different ways, maybe in different things, but everyone is learning. The most important thing that we can learn about ourselves and about others is that we can get along and that we can be community.

Our families wanted us to have an education. In the residential school, there was a sense of "we-they." It was painful. We were on the outside; we never really felt a part of it. I knew I needed to complete the educational process, but I felt like I was in a completely different world from the one I knew so well.

In some ways, being there gave me a chance to think about and see what was going on around me. Sometimes I did it very quietly, by detaching from everything that was happening around me. I looked at society and looked at myself. It gave me a perspective on things. As long as one has enough positive reinforcement of one's worth, one can survive that isolation.

❧

When I was in Grade 12, I knew I wanted to go to university. This was what I had always intended, but the principal . . . did not believe that I had the capacity to go on. Indian Affairs did not consider me as a suitable candidate for university, but suggested teacher training as more appropriate. As I had no money for advanced education, I felt compelled to take teacher training in Winnipeg.

Throughout residential school and arts and theology, I felt I was doing what needed to be done to be accepted and acceptable under the label of "education." Yet I didn't feel connected with what I was learning. In arts, for example, I was expected to listen to a lecture, then describe how I had understood it. I was expected to incorporate, regurgitate, then pass.

We spent the first part of the year in sociology memorizing terms. The sociological theories were all American concepts. They did not seem relevant to either Canadian or Aboriginal–Canadian concepts. I was really frustrated by this. I believed that a study of "society," of "sociology," should help me to understand what my friends and family were experiencing. This was in the late 1960s. Through my family, I was involved in the Friendship Centre movement. I knew and understood as an Aboriginal person that there were serious injustices in the Aboriginal community. I couldn't see any way that abstract sociological studies connected to justice issues and to the real world.

I was also frustrated by the fact that, in my twenty to twenty-five years of formal education, spiritual issues were never dealt with. This was true also of theological studies. One could graduate and be ordained without really working out the balance of spirituality in one's life.

To value only academic learning and accomplishment is to devalue experiential learning. There is a fundamental problem here. We need to value experience as highly as academic development. Many are silenced and oppressed because the academic has been seen as the only way to approach theology. We need to include everyone; everyone is gifted. Everyone can be affirmed. Within the Aboriginal community, we start with experiential learning. When we do this, we risk the critical eye of those whose experience is entirely academic and who measure by an academic model. They ask, "Is it real? Is it relevant?"

I quickly learned to love academic learning. I enjoyed Keats and Shakespeare and Chaucer. This was learning of another culture. It was valuable to learn another element of thought, another way of thinking. Yet, it was part of a trance-like existence. I really couldn't go back to an Aboriginal community and quote Chaucer. I was walking in a world, unaware of how I could connect with what I was learning. There was a question of who I really was and what I really believed. I was traveling without memory.

My quest for graduation and for ordination was something I questioned. The United Church was a powerful union of the Methodist, Presbyterian, and Congregational Churches. From my perspective in the Aboriginal community, the church was a place of power and privilege. Some clergypersons assume that they carry a lot of importance. It has become increasingly clear that there has been a great deal of abuse of power by people serving as counselors, pastors, and priests in our communities. This is a long-term issue that is only beginning to be faced. Paternalistic attitudes continue as a legacy from the colonial process.

I graduated from theology in late winter of 1971. Around the time I was graduating, the chairman of the Conference Settlement Committee of the United Church telephoned and asked to see me. He wanted to talk to me about my plans for the future and listed four or five communities in the north to which I could go. This was overwhelming for me. There were so many choices. When he mentioned Norway House, I immediately felt that this was where I wanted to go.

Just before my ordination, I was aware that I felt a tremendous call to ministry. I had no sense, however, of where my call might take me. I knew as an Aboriginal person that this was a doorway. I could use it as an opportunity to find a way to go about creative leadership in the life of the church. Ordination was a sign of the approval of the church. When I pause and think of the sense of being "set apart" that ordination implies, it is really problematic, coming out of a tribal community with egalitarian understanding. The image of being set apart and having special status really posed a problem.

I requested that my ordination take place in the community of Fisher River. The fact that my ordination was shared with my community made it somehow acceptable to me.

そ

When the Christian message was shared, the culture was denied. Yet the value system was not destroyed. The faith became real to me when I saw the ability of the church as community to respond to tragedy as it did in Norway House.

Community life was based on sharing. There was sharing of food, of life itself. Prior to refrigeration, when a deer or moose was killed, the meat was shared. In Norway House, the value system was still there, especially in the extended family. By then, the community was too large for this to work. Among the extended family, however, among cousins and aunts and uncles, it was still working. I kept expecting to see the spontaneous feasting and celebrations re-emerging.

Forty years ago when I was small, the economy in Fisher River was still alive. People still had dignity. When the game and fish were gone and welfare began, there were rations. The day came, however, when Indian Affairs recommended that there not be any feasting because it was considered wasteful. Usually the people gave up these ceremonies and other traditions of sharing, but sharing food is a real key to the value system.

The main thing that people need day by day is food. It's faithful to feed one another. It's faithful to share what is available, not to have a lot in storage. Out of small kitchens, people are served at every funeral, every night during the wake. There is never any shortage of food at those time. But things have changed. This is where our communities have suffered most. There have been many rites of passage, such as "naming" ceremonies and vision quests, which have been almost lost.

It is only two generations ago that many communities were disrupted and the value system began to be undermined. I saw that many moved away from building their own homes with their own resources. They didn't really contribute at all to the little shacks that were built and called home. There was really no involvement. People lost their dignity and spirit.

In Fisher River, massive changes happened all at once. The main changes, however, hinged on the building of the road. This increased contact with the outside community. Although the community understood itself to be in crisis, it had its own food and economic base; people built their own homes. Even under the umbrella of Indian Affairs, the community retained its integrity. Within one generation, the culmination of historic influences took away the dignity of the people: the flooding of the lands; destruction of the fisheries; and the conflict between the values of what my father refers to as the "dominant" society or the "competitive" society and the cultural values of the community.

こ。

In Aboriginal communities, there are two ways of surviving abuse and oppression. One way to survive is with inner strength, with "living in silence." This is a waiting for justice, living with a quiet hopefulness that some day this will end. This patient, spiritual passing of time in silence is something I've observed taking place throughout the whole culture. In a strange way, reservation life, being "set apart" in communities in which there is some shared life, has allowed this to continue.

I could look at my time going through residential school, through the teaching time, through arts and theology, as "doing what the man says." I did that knowing it wasn't going to destroy me. Principalities and powers cannot destroy the spirit if there is an element of strength there. There is a prophetic legend within the Aboriginal community called "The Seventh Fire." It tells us that "for six generations there will be oppression and the people will suffer greatly. With the lighting of the seventh fire, in the seventh generation, there will be a new age. Aboriginal people will find themselves and they will remember." I believe the seventh fire has been lit. Perhaps our children will be the ones who will break free from the oppression.

The prolonged silence has become unhealthy. The high rate of suicide, especially among our young people, reflects anger that is not being expressed in creative ways. Within the justice system and the wider society of Canada, the long silence has been unbroken to the point of our dying. Our young people are dying with tremendous cries of pain because, up to now, there has been no real sense of hope of another way.

It is important for oppressed peoples to break the silence for this is the way to liberation. My years in Norway House were a breaking of silence. I was filled with rage and outbursts at Presbytery meetings. It was so difficult to make people aware of how the continual lack of affirmation of the gifts of the people, of their offerings in the midst of the oppression they lived, affected community life.

In dealing with one's own anger, one must express it and not lose hope. When I deal cross-culturally, the hardest part for me is dealing with my own racism. I have an overwhelming respect for those who have kept silence in a good way. The Elders would say, "Don't attack someone to heal your own spirit." This fundamental respect for others is the Christ. Bearing the suffering of the people can be life-giving. My understanding that it is so is why it is possible for me to still be a Christian.

こ。

Something can be built from the image of the dry bones. There is a real need to be respectful and humble in visioning of community. It is important that people don't give up on themselves and on others. The prophetic saying, "Without a vision, the people die," emphasizes the need for vision. There needs to be a naming of the problem, followed by a dream or vision of what it might be to be whole.

Healing happens in the context of community. In the Aboriginal tradition, part of the vision of wholeness calls for balance. One must confront the problem and deal not only with the victims of violence and abuse but also create opportunities for the victimizers to find healing.

The Aboriginal way of healing in cases of abuse is an interesting attempt to bring a balanced approach to the problem. Victims are worked with principally, but not to the exclusion of victimizers. When a community can define its own healing, there is an opportunity for both victims and victimizers to be healed. The community won't be further fragmented. The healing of community is dynamic and allows us all to find healing and to be "healers." The key is balance.

To be Aboriginal and Christian implies being non-judgmental. There is a recognition that we are all in need of healing. This approach is much more holistic than individual therapy and counseling alone. Healing happens in the context of community. Valuing of culture is an important matter. In the midst of flux and change, a key is in the area of recognizing and naming what it is that is wrong and moving in the direction of healing.

᠅

There are gifts from each of the peoples in the four directions of the world. The winds of the different directions remind us of these gifts. The east represents the yellow-skinned peoples of the world. This direction symbolizes new life on the earth and reminds us of our connectedness to creation. The sun rises in the east; each day is a gift; life itself is a gift. South represents warmth and growth. This direction represents women, the doorway to life. The colour of the south is black, representing the black-skinned peoples of the world. West, symbolized by the color red, represents the gift of rest, the passing of time and of those who have gone before. Aboriginal peoples of the earth are symbolized in this direction. North is symbolized by the colour white, and represents coolness and the white-skinned people of the world. A gift of this direction is clarity of vision and a sense of the strength we need to live each day.

There was hope in the way this was taught. Every time I am in the lodge, I am reminded of the four directions. For me, the important part of this teaching is that this is the time of fulfillment. It is our task to learn of the interconnectedness of the winds. This is a hope-filled prophesy that is open to ongoing interpretation in our lives.

The four winds coming together connects with the struggle to be Aboriginal and Christian. It is holistic, reminding us that God so loved the world. The teaching of the four winds helps us overcome the racism and sexism that has existed in the Christian church.

Donald Ng

Donald Ng's passages, from his essay in The Ongoing Journey: Awakening Spiritual Life in At-Risk Youth, *provide just a hint of the vast complexity of Asian-American culture, as well as glimpses of his own life as a Chinese-American. The Reverend Ng is Director of Education for Discipleship of the American Baptist Churches.*

A computer expert, a scientist, a math student, a martial arts master, a Chinese restaurant worker, a foreigner, a foreign student, an immigrant, a Japanese businessman or tourist. A person who is quiet, shy, won't speak up in groups, plays tennis or Ping Pong, speaks with an accent, knows where the best Chinese restaurants are, knows the whereabouts of any Asian person living in his or her home city, has ancestors from some faraway land in the Orient.

These are just a few of the most common perceptions people might have when they see or meet an Asian American person. When we think of Asians, a multiplicity of images come to mind. We may think of nationalities, language groups, regional homelands, generational categories, facial features, physique and pigmentation characteristics, and many other images.

The term "Asian American" represents a very diverse group of people There are Burmese, Cambodian, Chinese, Filipino, Hmong, Indian, Indonesian, Japanese, Korean, Laotian, Malaysian, Mien, Pacific Islanders, Singaporean, Thai, Vietnamese, and others. Although the experiences of some of the groups may be similar, each has a distinct culture, language, and history.

Today, Asian Americans belong to the fastest-growing ethnic minority group in the United States. According to John Naisbitt's *Trend Letter* (May 10, 1990), "Asian Americans skyrocketed from 3.7 million residents in 1980 to more than 6.5 million today, a 71 percent increase—seven times the general population expansion. By the year 2000, four of every 100 U.S. residents will be Asian Americans. Bolstered by a continuing immigration wave through this decade, the number of Japanese, Chinese, Filipinos, Koreans, Vietnamese, Cambodians, and other Asian residents will exceed 10 million in the new millennium"

Here are some startling facts from Naisbitt:

- California, the nation's gateway to the booming Pacific Rim and home to nearly 3 million Asian Americans, has the largest concentration.
- Half of Monterey Park's residents are of Chinese descent.
- The world's largest Korean community outside Korea can be found in Los Angeles. Some 300,000 Koreans live in the city's Koreantown.
- If you look in San Jose's phone book, you'll find far more people named Nguyen, a Vietnamese surname, than Jones.

In addition to the dramatic population growth of Asian Americans that has caught the attention of the media, Asian Americans are said to be more affluent, on the average, than any other racial or ethnic group, including whites. Furthermore, Asians have been credited with having the highest level of education of all other groups: Among adults 25 or older, 14 percent of Asians have five or more years of college, compared with only 9 percent of all Americans. Although these statistics are marveled at by entrepreneurs for new markets and misused to create a "model minority" myth, there are many exceptions and particularities to those figures that raise questions about the validity of these assertions.

For example, one exception to the above statistics is the validity of understanding Asian Americans as a monolithic group. Usually, the non-Asian, for whatever reason, would prefer to treat all Asians alike. Subsequently, there has been increasing media coverage on the identify of Asian Americans as a group. Susmu Awanohara of Los Angeles, writing in the *Far Eastern Review*, said:

The sheer heterogeneity of Asian Americans makes it hard for them to consolidate political power. They are divided into at least half a dozen major ethnic groups, each of which is further subdivided according to the time of arrival, social origins, religious and factional affiliations.

The nomenclature of "Asian Americans" was first introduced in the 1960s for advocating legislation favoring the interests of Asians. By grouping together, Asians had political clout to petition for census-driven policy-making, leading to the establishment of affirmative-action goals and federal aid to Asian American communities. Although the name is being used more today, most people do not call themselves Asian Americans except for the reasons stated earlier. In most cases, they tend to describe themselves in specific, rather than general, terms.

I am a second-generation Chinese American. In the Chinese culture, we have an acronym—ABC. It doesn't refer only to the American Baptist Churches; it also refers to American-Born Chinese. It would be even more derogatory for a Chinese elder to call me Jook Sing instead of Ju Gak. Jook is the Chinese word for bamboo, and Jook Sing is the hollow part of the bamboo. As you cut the bamboo in half, there are hollow sections. But every now and then, usually a foot apart, there are knots, and Ju Gak means "the knot." Jook Sing means "the hollow part." Now they call me Jook Sing because I was born in the United States. Even though I look Asian on the outside, I'm hollow on the inside—I don't appreciate my Chinese traditions and rituals. Those who are born in Asia are referred to as Jook Gak because they are both Asian on the outside as well as Asian on the inside.

Our self-descriptions are further complicated by likes and dislikes, experiences, interests, abilities, skills, vocation, etc. For example, as a Chinese American, I can neither read nor write Chinese. but I can still speak Toisanese with my mother. Sometimes, I feel I can't read, write, or even speak English any better! As a Chinese American, I can wolf down a hot dog and Coke in Fenway Park as well as pick the meat off oxtails stewed in black beans and drink a cup of chrysanthemum tea in my mother's house. . . .

The histories of Asian Americans are rooted in America's developing national identity and expanding economic needs. To understand why Asian Americans came to the United States, you must first understand that there is both a national identity issue as well as an economic issue. On the one hand, Asian laborers have been deliberately sought to meet the growing needs of American businesses. On the other hand, Asians have been perceived as inhuman or subhuman, a threat to racial purity, un-American, and unassimilable. . . .

America's changing perception of Asians, or for that matter of any racial/ethnic group, is based on America's self-identity and the process known as "Americanization." Throughout U.S. history, there have been different policies in the Americanizing of new immigrants and racial/ethnic people. According to Philip Gleason, in an article in the *Harvard Encyclopedia of Racial Ethnic Groups*, it was an ideological quality that was important during the colonial period in determining the definition of an American identity. According to Gleason:

To be or become American, a person did not have to be of any particular national, linguistic, religious, or ethnic background. All he had to do was to commit himself to the political ideology centered on the abstract ideals of liberty, equality and republicanism.

In the first half of the 1800s, a large influx of European immigrants who were Roman Catholics created bitter bursts of nativism. Organized political efforts to secure public funds to support Catholic education was perhaps the most highly charged issue of all. In order to protect their religion from nativistic attacks, it was imperative for Catholics to distinguish between nationality and the Catholic faith, so that immigrants would not abandon their faith in the process of Americanization. To be Catholic is not to be un-American.

In the latter half of the 1800s, we begin to see the elements of race and ethnicity becoming central to the discussion of nationality. This was the period when large numbers of Chinese immigrants arrived in the United States.

I've already mentioned that I am an American-born Chinese. I also should mention that my parents are from China and that my father served in the U.S. Army during World War II after coming to the United States. He left my mother and older brother in China and came to the United States to work and have enough economic success so that he could eventually return to China to live out the rest of his life. The other point I want to make is that both my paternal and maternal grandfathers worked in the United States as laborers and they too left their families in China. This was a very common way for Chinese to immigrate to the United States. It is interesting that a lot of people say to us, "Why don't you go home to where you came from?" Well, my grandparents, as well as my father, really had no intentions to stay here, but the turn of history almost made it impossible for them to return. My father actually was drafted by the United States Army during World War II and served as a corporal in Germany. Eventually, because he served honorably in the United States Army, he became a citizen and then was able to sponsor my mother and older brother so they could come to the United States. That is some personal history about how some Chinese came to the States.

Traci West

Traci West, writing from the perspective of an African American woman, suggests that the concept "diversity" is increasingly being used as a crutch by European Americans in order to evade the stark reality of continuing and entrenched racism. "I Am NOT Your Diversity" appeared in The Other Side, *July-August 1994. Dr. West is Assistant Professor of Theology at Drew University, Madison, New Jersey.*

I think the term "diversity" is a popular racial euphemism that needs reexamining. In fact, the word is so broadly applied that I am almost ready to call a moratorium on its use. Weighted with the best of intentions, pronouncements about diversity in liberal, predominantly White, local and national churches abound. Catch phrases like "a concern for increasing our diversity," "the importance of celebrating our diversity," or "a need to train and sensitize people to better cope with diversity" are everywhere.

It is indeed a unique occurrence in the United States when people from a range of ethnic and racial backgrounds gather together under a single denominational banner or ecumenical agency. There is certainly something intrinsically good about cultural exchange, to whatever extent it takes place at ethnically and racially diverse gatherings.

Nevertheless, I recommend extreme caution when we promote, create, or celebrate "diversity." Too often, underlying the desire for diversity is the ironic goal of perpetuating a notion of sameness. Celebrating diversity cultivates the therapeutic sentiment that everyone in our society has an equitable social identity because we each have some kind of unique cultural heritage.

Such a scenario is false. We are not all the same. When the term "diversity" is used as a generalization to connote sameness, it conveys the notion that the experiences of all ethnic and racial groups in the United States are virtually interchangeable.

Too often, a focus on diversity prevents us from confronting racism, or, more specifically, White supremacy. White supremacy is the most common form of racism found in the history and culture of the United States. Evidence of the continuing power of White supremacy is manifested in crises spanning health problems, such as infant mortality and malnutrition, to environmental decisions about the choice of neighborhood sites for dumping waste products. . . .

Exclusive focus on diversity ignores the imbalance of structural power and privilege concentrated in the hands of White people. Because of the institutionalized political, economic, and cultural power that Whites hold in this country, we are *not* all the same. When my White friend walks into a clothing store, a corporate boardroom, or a classroom, she benefits from the fact that radically different assumptions, based on a privileged racial status, are made about her than are made about me when I, an African American, walk into the same places.

In addition, I am shocked by the blatant objectification operative in references to diversity. On more than one occasion, I have been invited to participate in church-sponsored events with the explanation: "We want you to speak because we really want to have diversity." I hardly feel flattered by such tokenism. If I do participate in the event, despite the offensive invitation, I wear a wonderful button designed by the Women's Theological Center in Boston that says, "I am NOT your diversity."

The term "diversity" is often simply White-liberalspeak meaning that one or more persons of color are present at a worship service or meeting. Supposedly, this heralds some kind of significant social breakthrough. Yet focusing exclusively on the goal of diversity facilitates a short-term catharsis without confronting the racism of our society. As a result, White people avoid accusations of racism because there is "diversity." Similarly, persons of color can feel they make a contribution merely because their presence provides a degree of "diversity."

Racial and ethnic diversity, especially in religious settings, is a laudable and important first step. But in light of the multiple current crises in our country perpetuated by structural racism, the church and broader society must move beyond celebrations of diversity. We must ask ourselves: Are we willing to identify and combat the immoral, White supremacist underpinnings of societal inequity? Is anyone willing to adopt explicitly anti-racist agendas and policies?

In several recent public appearances, civil-rights attorney and law professor Lani Guinier has urged the Clinton administration to convene a summit to follow up the 1968 Kerner Commission report on racial issues in the United States. At a conference of African American women academics in Boston earlier this year, she reiterated some of the ways her ideas and strategies on civil rights had been distorted and misrepresented, causing President Clinton to rescind her nomination for a position in the Justice Department. Among public officials who resist addressing issues of racism, Guinier commented, " 'race' has become a new four-letter word."

Along with Guinier, I contend that specific attention to understanding and eliminating racism has been diverted. Too often, emphasis on diversity has supplanted an ability to talk directly about race. The drive to stress diversity contributes to an ethos where naming and confronting the particular problems that result from racial inequities and prejudice is almost tantamount to uttering profanity.

The idea of struggle is always tough to embrace. It is far easier to champion the cause of diversity rather than commit to confronting racism, for the same reason that few people traditionally attend Maundy Thursday worship service but pack the church on Easter Sunday. Likewise, we celebrate the birthday of Dr. Martin Luther King, Jr., in January (in most places) and forget to honor the day of his assassination in April. Merely talking about sacrificial, risky behavior is hard for most of us to tolerate. We can expect that challenging White supremacy in our institutions and ourselves will involve direct conflict and prolonged critical examination. The process is indeed arduous, but politically—and morally—correct.

Peggy McIntosh

Peggy McIntosh is careful to point out that she speaks as one white woman in one particular situation. **"White Privilege: Unpacking the Invisible Knapsack"** *is her attempt to respond to the entrenched racism in our society and in her particular professional realm. Dr. McIntosh is Associate Director of the Wellesley College Center for Research on Women. She has lectured and written extensively on women's and multicultural issues.*

Through work to bring materials from Women's Studies into the rest of the curriculum, I have often noticed men's unwillingness to grant that they are over-privileged, even though they may grant that women are disadvantaged. They may say they will work to improve women's status, in the society, the university, or the curriculum, but they can't or won't support the idea of lessening men's. Denials which amount to taboos surround the subject of advantages which men gain from women's disadvantages. These denials protect male privilege from being fully acknowledged, lessened or ended.

Thinking through unacknowledged male privilege as a phenomenon, I realized that since hierarchies in our society are interlocking, there was most likely a phenomenon of white privilege which was similarly denied and protected. As a white person, I realized I had been taught about racism as something which puts others at a disadvantage, but had been taught not to see one of its corollary aspects, white privilege, which puts me at an advantage.

I think whites are carefully taught not to recognize white privilege, as males are taught not to recognize male privilege. So I have begun in an untutored way to ask what it is like to have white privilege. I have come to see white privilege as an invisible package of unearned assets which I can count on cashing in each day, but about which I was 'meant' to remain oblivious. White privilege is like an invisible weightless knapsack of special provisions, maps, passports, codebooks, visas, clothes, tools and blank checks.

Describing white privilege makes one newly accountable. As we in Women's Studies work to reveal male privilege and ask men to give up some of their power, so one who writes about having white privilege must ask, "Having described it, what will I do to lessen or end it?"

After I realized the extent to which men work from a base of unacknowledged privilege, I understood that much of their oppressiveness was unconscious. Then I remembered the frequent charges from women of color that white women whom they encounter are oppressive. I began to understand why we are justly seen as oppressive, even when we don't see ourselves that way. I began to count the ways in which I enjoy unearned skin-color privilege and have been conditioned into oblivion about its existence.

My schooling gave me no training in seeing myself as an oppressor, as an unfairly advantaged person, or as a participant in a damaged culture. I was taught to see myself as an individual whose moral state depended on her individual moral will. My schooling followed the pattern my colleague Elizabeth Minnich has pointed out: whites are taught to think of their lives as morally neutral, normative, and average, and also ideal, so that when we work to benefit others, this is seen as work which will allow "them" to be more like "us."

I decided to try to work on myself at least by identifying some of the daily effects of white privilege in my life. I have chosen those conditions which I think in my case *attach somewhat more to skin-color privilege* than to class, religion, ethnic status, or geographical location, though of course all these other factors are intricately intertwined. As far as I can see, my African American co-workers, friends and acquaintances with whom I come into daily or frequent contact in this particular time, place, and line of work cannot count on most of these conditions.

1. I can if I wish arrange to be in the company of people of my race most of the time.
2. If I should need to move, I can be pretty sure of renting or purchasing housing in an area which I can afford and in which I would want to live.
3. I can be pretty sure that my neighbors in such a location will be neutral or pleasant to me.
4. I can go shopping alone most of the time, pretty well assured that I will not be followed or harassed.
5. I can turn on the television or open to the front page of the paper and see people of my race widely represented.
6. When I am told about our national heritage or about "civilization," I

am shown that people of my color made it what it is.

7. I can be sure that my children will be given curricular materials that testify to the existence of their race.
8. If I want to, I can be pretty sure of finding a publisher for this piece on white privilege.
9. I can go into a music shop and count on finding the music of my race represented, into a supermarket and find the staple foods which fit with my cultural traditions, into a hairdresser's shop and find someone who can cut my hair.
10. Whether I use checks, credit cards, or cash, I can count on my skin color not to work against the appearance of financial reliability.
11. I can arrange to protect my children most of the time from people who might not like them.
12. I can swear, or dress in second-hand clothes, or not answer letters, without having people attribute these choices to the bad morals, the poverty, or the illiteracy of my race.
13. I can speak in public to a powerful male group without putting my race on trial.
14. I can do well in a challenging situation without being called a credit to my race.
15. I am never asked to speak for all the people of my racial group.
16. I can remain oblivious of the language and customs of persons of color who constitute the world's majority without feeling in my culture any penalty for such oblivion.
17. I can criticize our government and talk about how much I fear its policies and behavior without being seen as a cultural outsider.
18. I can be pretty sure that if I ask to talk to "the person in charge," I will be facing a person of my race.
19. If a traffic cop pulls me over or if the IRS audits my tax return, I can be sure I haven't been singled out because of my race.
20. I can easily buy posters, postcards, picture books, greeting cards, dolls, toys, and children's magazines featuring people of my race.
21. I can go home from most meetings of organizations I belong to feeling somewhat tied in, rather than isolated, out-of-place, outnumbered, unheard, held at a distance, or feared.
22. I can take a job with an affirmative-action employer without having co-workers on the job suspect that I got it because of my race.
23. I can choose public accommodation without fearing that people of my race cannot get in or will be mistreated in the places I have chosen.
24. I can be sure that if I need legal or medical help, my race will not work against me.
25. If my day, week, or year is going badly, I need not ask of each negative episode or situation whether it has racial overtones.
26. I can choose blemish cover or bandages in "flesh" color and have them more or less match my skin.

I repeatedly forgot each of the realizations on this list until I wrote it down. For me white privilege has turned out to be an elusive and fugitive subject. The pressure to avoid it is great, for in facing it I must give up the myth of meritocracy. If these things are true, this is not such a free country; one's life is not what one makes it; many doors open for certain people through no virtues of their own.

In unpacking this invisible knapsack of white privilege, I have listed conditions of daily experience which I once took for granted. Nor did I think of any of these perquisites as bad for the holder. I now think that we need a more finely differentiated taxonomy of privilege, for some of these varieties are only what one would want for everyone in a just society, and others give license to be ignorant, oblivious, arrogant and destructive.

I see a pattern running through the matrix of white privilege, a pattern of assumptions which were passed on to me as a white person. There was one main piece of cultural turf; it was my own turf, and I was among those who could control the turf. *My skin color was an asset for any move I was educated to want to make.* I could think of myself as belonging in major ways, and of making social systems work for me. I could freely disparage, fear, neglect, or be oblivious to anything outside of the dominant cultural forms. Being of the main culture, I could also criticize it fairly freely.

In proportion as my racial group was being made confident, comfortable, and oblivious, other groups were likely being made inconfident, uncomfortable, and alienated. Whiteness protected me from many kinds of hostility, distress, and violence, which I was being subtly trained to visit in turn upon people of color.

For this reason, the word "privilege" now seems to me misleading. We usually think of privilege as being a favored state, whether earned or conferred by birth or luck. Yet some of the conditions I have described here work to systematically overempower certain groups. Such privilege simply *confers dominance* because of one's race or sex.

I want, then, to distinguish between earned strength and unearned power conferred systemically. Power from unearned privilege can look like strength when it is in fact permission to escape or to dominate. But not all of the privileges on my list are inevitably damaging. Some, like the expectation that neighbors will be decent to you, or that your race will not count against you in court, should be the norm in a just society. Others, like the privilege to ignore less powerful people, distort the humanity of the holders as well as the ignored groups.

We might at least start by distinguishing between positive advantages which we can work to spread, and negative types of advantages which unless rejected will always reinforce our present hierarchies. For example, the feeling that one belongs within the human circle, as Native Americans say, should not be seen as privilege for a few. Ideally it is an *unearned entitlement*. At present, since only a few have it, it is an *unearned advantage* for them. This paper results from a process of coming to see that some of the power which I originally saw as attendant on being a human being in the U.S. consisted in *unearned advantage* and *conferred dominance*.

I have met very few men who are truly distressed about systemic, unearned male advantage and conferred dominance. And so one question for me and others like me is whether we will be like them, or whether we will get truly distressed, even outraged, about unearned race advantage and conferred dominance and, if so, what we will do to lessen them. In any case, we need to do more work in identifying how they actually affect our daily lives. Many, perhaps most, of our white students in the U.S. think that racism doesn't affect them because they are not people of color; they do not see "whiteness" as a racial identity. In addition, since race and sex are not the only advantaging systems at work, we need similarly to examine the daily experience of having age advantage, or ethnic advantage, or physical ability, or advantage related to nationality, religion, or sexual orientation.

Difficulties and dangers surrounding the task of finding parallels are many. Since racism, sexism, and heterosexism are not the same, the advantaging associated with them should not be seen as the same. In addition, it is hard to disentangle aspects of unearned advantage which rest more on social class, economic class, race, religion, sex and ethnic identity than on other factors. Still, all of the oppressions are interlocking, as the Combahee River Collective Statement of 1977 continues to remind us eloquently.

One factor seems clear about all of the interlocking oppressions. They take both active forms which we can see and embedded forms which as a member of the dominant group one is taught not to see. In my class and place, I did not see myself as a racist because I was taught to recognize racism only in individual acts of meanness by members of my group, never in invisible systems conferring unsought racial dominance on my group from birth.

Disapproving of the systems won't be enough to change them. I was taught to think that racism could end if white individuals changed their attitudes. [But] a "white" skin in the United States opens many doors for whites whether or not we approve of the way dominance has been conferred on us. Individual acts can palliate, but cannot end, these problems.

To redesign social systems we need first to acknowledge their colossal unseen dimensions. The silences and denials surrounding privilege are the key political tool here. They keep the thinking about equality or equity incomplete, protecting unearned advantage and conferred dominance by making these taboo subjects. Most talk by whites about equal opportunity seems to me now to be about equal opportunity to try to get into a position of dominance while denying that *systems* of dominance exist.

It seems to me that obliviousness about white advantage, like obliviousness about male advantage, is kept strongly inculturated in the United States so as to maintain the myth of meritocracy, the myth that democratic choice is equally available to all. Keeping most people unaware that freedom of confident action is there for just a small number of people props up those in power, and serves to keep power in the hands of the same groups that have most of it already.

Though systemic change takes many decades, there are pressing questions for me and I imagine for some others like me if we raise our daily consciousness on the perquisites of being light-skinned. What will we do with such knowledge? As we know from watching men, it is an open question whether we will choose to use unearned advantage to weaken hidden systems of advantage, and whether we will use any of our arbitrarily awarded power to try to reconstruct power systems on a broader base.

Part Two
REEXAMING THE PAST: HOW DID WE GET HERE?

At the start of an interview with representatives of a multicultural congregation, presented in the final section of this book, someone posed the following challenge to the interviewer: "You know, of course, that by framing the questions you are setting the terms of this conversation." And the speaker was entirely correct, though in this instance, happily, the interview turned out to be a free-ranging conversation with little direction from the interviewer. Yet, the comment goes directly to the core of efforts such as this book. By selecting certain materials, one is setting certain directions. Unhappily, short of doing nothing at all, this is inevitable. What, then, is the purpose of this collection? In the view of the editor, it is to present as many strong, diverse voices as possible—voices that need to be heard, digested, discussed, acted upon. They are very different voices, at times stating differing, even conflicting, opinions, but they all contribute to the important underlying issue: development of a harmonious, functioning society—one that provides sufficient room for every member and group within that society to live and develop freely and fully.

We begin this section with an essay by George Tinker, a theologian of Osage Indian and Norwegian parentage, who presents a forceful analysis of the European American missionary enterprise in the United States seen, so to speak, through the lens of its victims. The next selection is Katie Geneva Cannon's examination of America's slave history, seen through the prism of her African American ancestors. Richard Rodriguez, writer and television commentator, writes vividly and movingly of his parents' life as Mexican immigrants in the California of the 1950s. Finally, Mary Swander, a poet and novelist, reminds us that "European American" is a term that, in itself, covers a wide-ranging diversity which has led to its own variety and richness, as well as intergroup tensions, within Canada and the United States.

George E. Tinker

George E. Tinker, of Osage and Norwegian parentage, analyzes with unsparing directness, yet generosity of spirit, the American mission-ary enterprise as experienced by those who were, so to speak, its helpless victims. Our excerpt comes from **Missionary Conquest: The Gospel and Native American Cultural Genocide.** *Dr. Tinker, a Lutheran theologian, is Associate Professor of Cross-Cultural Min-istries at Iliff School of Theology, Denver, Colorado, and Pastor of Living Waters Episcopal/Lutheran Indian Ministry.*

This [work] . . . is about Indian people in North America and the Christian missionaries who devoted their lives to Indian evangelization. It is a story filled with pathos, energy, suffering, and even romance, when told by the missionaries and their biographers or historians. All too often in telling this story, well-meaning authors hyperbolize the romantic as-pects of a missionary's work but include little of critical substance. The biographies of missionaries tend to be much closer in form to that medi-eval genre of hagiography (that is, the life of a saint) than to post-Enlight-enment analytical historiography.

Told from an Indian perspective, the story is far less entertaining and much less endearing. Pain and devastation become dominant elements as Indian anger erupts to the surface. Indeed, today the white missionary, both in the historical memory of Indian people and in the contemporary experience, has become a frequent target of scorn in most segments of the Indian world. Many implicitly recognize some connection between Indian suffering and the missionary presence, even as they struggle to make sense not only of past wrongs, but also of the pain of contemporary Indian existence. The pain experienced by Indians today is readily apparent in too many statistics that put Indians on the top or bottom of lists. For instance, Indian people suffer the lowest per capita income of any ethnic group in the United States, the highest teenage suicide rate, a 60 percent unemployment rate nationally, and a scandalously low longevity that re-mains below sixty years for both men and women.

Yet even in the contemporary Indian world, there is no common un-derstanding of this history. On the one hand, the old traditional ways have enjoyed a revival over the past twenty years. This revival has been fueled in part by anger over generations of oppression suffered at the hands of white civilization and its institutions. The latter include Chris-tian churches as well as educational, economic and political institutions. As a part of this larger movement, the return to traditional Indian reli-gions is an exercise in self-determination and not just a product of anger at memories or current experiences of missionary history as a cultural imposition. Most Indian people in North America have been Christian-ized, however, even if only nominally. A good portion of Indian people have been Christian for several generations, and more than a few are very faithful to the denominations into which they have been evange-lized. Furthermore, Indian congregations quite commonly remain faithful not only to the denomination, but to the very missionary theology that was first brought to them even when the denomination has long ago abandoned that language for a more contemporary articulation of the

Endnotes

1. See Ashis Nandy, *The Intimate Enemy: Loss and Recovery of Self under Colonial-ism* (Delhi: Oxford Univ. Press, 1983), v, xv, 2, 7.

.2. See Clyde A. Milner, *With Good Intentions: Quaker Work among the Pawnees, Otos, and Omahas in the 1870s* (Lincoln: Univ. of Nebraska Press, gospel. One must at least suspect that the process of Christianization has involved some internalization of the larger illusion of Indian inferiority and the idealization of white culture and religion. Some have called it internalized racism, and as such it surely results in a praxis of self-hatred.[1]

What I am describing should surprise no one. The phenomenon is part of a much broader process that can be seen in other aspects of human existence. Just as an abused child slowly but inevitably internalizes a parent's abuse as a consistent demonstration of the child's own shortcomings and may even regard the life of the abusive parent as exemplary, so communities of oppressed peoples internalize their own oppression and come to believe too many of the stereotypes, explicit and implicit, spoken by the oppressor. . . .

To state the case baldly and dramatically, my thesis is that the Christian missionaries—of all denominations working among American Indian nations—were partners in genocide. Unwittingly no doubt, and always with the best of intentions, nevertheless the missionaries were guilty of complicity in the destruction of Indian cultures and tribal social structures—complicity in the devastating impoverishment and death of the people to whom they preached.[2] I will explore the extent to which each of these missionary heroes implicitly blurred any distinction between the gospel of salvation and their own culture. This blurring invariably resulted in the missionary's culture, values, and social and political structures, not to say political hegemony and control, being imposed on tribal peoples, all in the name of the gospel. That is to say, the kerygmatic content of the missionary's Christian faith became confused with the accoutrements of the missionary's cultural experience and behavior. It is important to my thesis that my selections are among the churches' most remembered and most revered missionaries, who have been the subjects of countless hagiographies and continue to serve as models. They have, I would argue, been elevated implicitly to the status of sainthood. My examples include John Eliot in Puritan New England, Pierre-Jean De Smet in the Northwest, soon to be officially "Saint" Junipero Serra in California, and Henry Benjamin Whipple, Episcopal bishop of Minnesota during the latter half of the nineteenth century.

I must stress that my point is not simply to criticize these departed heroes nor to punish their memory; nor do I wish to impose a burden of guilt on their existing denominations or heirs today.[3] Rather, I intend to expose the illusion, the covert "lie" of white self-righteousness as it was internalized and acted out by the missionaries themselves. I do this out of a sense that this is part of America's unfinished business. Tangentially, it becomes a contribution to our understanding of why Native American peoples have generally failed to enter the American mainstream and continue to live in poverty and oppression, marginalized on the periphery of society. By and large, Indian people have not found liberation in the gospel of Jesus Christ, but, rather, continued bondage to a culture that is both alien and alienating, and even genocidal against American Indian peoples.[4] Finally, in a conclusion I will bring many of these things together to try to explore their contemporary significance.

Cultural genocide is more subtle than overt military extermination, yet it is no less devastating to a people. Although the evidence is clear that Serra's missionary empire engaged in severe corporal punishment, there

1972), for a treatment of Quaker missionary involvement during the period of Whipple's activity. There was substantial Episcopal— Quaker cooperation during these years as both pursued the same reform goals; see Rayner Wickersham Kelsey, *Friends and the Indians: 1655–1917* (Philadelphia: Associated Executive Committee of Friends on Indian Affairs, 1917), 164ff.

3. I have selected representative examples from different main-line denominations to avoid the appearance of any bias toward a particular denomination. The only church notably absent is my own denomination. The Lutherans seem to have somewhat avoided these pitfalls. Namely, in the United States, Lutherans avoided much of the missionary zeal of other churches, preferring instead simply to displace Indian people and occupy the best Indian lands in Minnesota, Iowa, Kansas, and the Dakotas. This gentle barb aside, there were indeed a few Lutheran efforts, which invariably fell into the same Euroamerican pattern of cultural arrogance. See, for example, Gerhard M. Schmutterer, *Tomahawk and Cross: Lutheran Missionaries among the Northern Plains Tribes, 1858–1866* (Sioux Falls: Augustana College, 1989), whose hagiographic content is heralded in the dedication at the beginning of the volume: "Dedicated to the memory of Moritz Braeuninger, Lutheran missionary martyr in America. . . ." While many have assumed Braeuninger was murdered by Indians in 1860, he is just as likely to have been killed by a bear (p. 79) or drowned in the Powder River by accident. See also Erwin Fritschel, *A History of the Indian Mission of the Lutheran Iowa Synod, 1856 to 1866* (Fort Collins: Colo-

rado State College of Education, 1939); Albert Keiser, *Lutheran Missions among the American Indians* (Minneapolis: Augsburg, 1922); Adam Schuster, *Von Indianern ermordet* (Neuendettelsau: Missionsverlag, 1929); Schmutterer and Charles Lutz, "Iowa 1854: Mission Martyr on the Western Frontier: Can Cross-cultural Mission Be Achieved?" in *Church Roots*, ed. Charles Lutz (Minneapolis: Augsburg, 1985), 117–42; and Oswald F. Wagner, "Lutheran Zealots among the Crows," *Montana: The Magazine of Western History* 22 (1972): 2–19.

4. See George Tinker and Paul Schultz, *Rivers of Life; Native Spirituality for Native Churches* (Minneapolis: Augsburg Fortress, 1988), chaps. 1 and 2, for a discussion of modern reservation realities with regard to Indian dysfunctionality and church participation.

5. Sherburne F. Cook, *The Conflict between the California Indian and White Civilization* (Berkeley: Univ. of California Press, 1976 [orig. 1943]); and Rupert and Jeanne Costo, eds., *The Missions of California: A Legacy of Genocide* (San Francisco: Indian Historian Press, 1987).

6. See Alfred W. Crosby, "Virgin Soil Epidemics as a Factor in the Aboriginal Depopulation in America," *William and Mary Quarterly*, 3d ser., 33 (1976: 289–99; Sherburne F. Cook, *The Indian Population of New England in the Seventeenth Century*, University of California Publications in Anthropology, no. 12 (Berkeley, 1976); and "The Significance of Disease in the Extinction of the New England Indians," *Human Biology* 45 (1973).

For American Indian scholarship on Indian demography, see Lenore A.

is certainly no evidence that missionaries ever engaged in the systematic killing of Indian people (with the exception, of course, of "Col." John Chivington at Sand Creek, who was a former missionary and the Methodist district superintendent in Denver when he volunteered for military service). Nevertheless, the Native American population of coastal California was reduced by some 90 percent during seventy years under the sole proprietorship of Serra's mission system.[5] Imported diseases, especially "virgin soil" epidemics, are usually cited as the cause for such devastating statistics.[6] Yet the effects of the European invasion on the culture, political structure, and economics of the people call for a thorough analysis of all the effects of the missions in California, including the extent to which the evangelizing effort weakened the native cultures so as to imperil the very survival of the people.

Cultural genocide can be defined as the effective destruction of a people by systematically or systemically (intentionally or unintentionally in order to achieve other goals) destroying, eroding, or undermining the integrity of the culture and system of values that defines a people and gives them life. First of all, it involves the destruction of those cultural structures of existence that give a people a sense of holistic and communal integrity. It does this by limiting a people's freedom to practice their culture and to live out their lives in culturally appropriate patterns. It effectively destroys a people by eroding both their self-esteem and the interrelationships that bind them together as a community. In North American mission history, cultural genocide almost always involved an attack on the spiritual foundations of a people's unity by denying the existing ceremonial and mythological sense of a community in relationship to the Sacred Other. Finally, it erodes a people's self-image as a whole people by attacking or belittling every aspect of native culture.

At least four interrelated vehicles can be used in coming to some understanding of cultural genocide. These four categories are patently artificial and certainly overlap extensively, but they may be helpful in understanding the complexities of cultural genocide. It needs to be repeated that cultural genocide is never the ultimate goal and quite often not the overt intention but results from the pursuit of some other goal of economic gain and political dominance.

1. The *political* aspects of cultural genocide involve the use of political means and political power, always with the threat of military or police intervention, by a more powerful political entity in order to control and subdue a weaker, culturally discrete entity. This constitutes genocide because it results in the loss not only of a people's political viability but also of their cultural viability.[7] The treaties signed by the United States with Indian nations were indeed a form of political genocide. They were invariably forced on Indian people who were offered little choice or alternative. Moreover, missionaries often aided government officials in these processes. The consistent failure of the United States to keep those treaty agreements is a further act of political/cultural genocide.[8] The "Civilization" Act passed by the U.S. Congress in 1819 was clearly an attempt to co-opt the churches and their missionaries to serve the government's political ends with respect to Indian peoples.[9] And the missionaries were only too glad to be co-opted for the sake of federal land grants and funding for mission schools. The so-called

Grant Peace Policy of the 1870s delegated to the denominations the responsibility for filling the positions of Indian agent, parceling out particular nations or reservations to various denominations.[10] The missionaries of all the churches came to Indian nations with the firm support of the political authorities. In Utah, for instance, the Mormon leader, Brigham Young, was called on to serve as U.S. Indian agent for the territory.[11] Even missionaries of the most revered memory regularly fell into complicity with the political impetus to conquest. In 1539 the governor of Guatemala, Alonso de Maldonado, wrote in great praise of the missionary outreach of Bartolomé de Las Casas and his value to the interests of the crown:

> Father Bartolomé de Las Casas and other religious here are succeeding in the peaceful conquest of this warlike territory. To this end they have been carrying on negotiations with the Indians, unknown to any Spaniard save themselves and me.[12]

Here a secular political authority acknowledges that the great friend of Indian people in the early Spanish conquest of the Americas also had conquest on his mind, even if he hoped to accomplish it without the brutality and bloodshed he witnessed on the part of his countrymen.

2. The *economic* aspects of genocide involve using or allowing the economic systems, always with political and even military support, to manipulate and exploit another culturally discrete entity that is both politically and economically weaker. The results can range from enslavement and the direct exploitation of labor to the pillaging of natural economic resources that leaves a people unable to sustain themselves. The eradication of the buffalo and the coincident federal establishment of the reservation system is an example of economic and political forms of cultural genocide functioning together to destroy the viability of Plains Indian cultures.[13] When Kit Carson destroyed the entire agricultural production of the Navajo people, he used an economic strategy to win a military victory and achieve their final subjugation.[14] The destruction of the crops caused immediate hunger; destruction of whole orchards meant long-term devastation.

3. *Religious* aspects of genocide involve the overt attempt to destroy the spiritual solidarity of a people. Sometimes this was done by outlawing ceremonial forms, as in the 1890 legislation that made performance of the plains Sun Dance and the Hopi Snake Dance, among others, a punishable crime.[15] At other times, military suppression was used, as in the case of the Ghost Dance. This resulted on one occasion in the massacre of some 350 people at Wounded Knee (December 29, 1890), including a great many women, children, and old people.[16] Most typically, however, the missionaries, emboldened by their sense of political and economic superiority, used preaching and the promised bliss of conversion to denounce or belittle native forms of prayer and argue their own spiritual superiority. Moreover, they used their influence to promote the 1890 legislation limiting freedom of religion for Indian peoples and implicitly "establishing" Christianity.[17]

4. The *social* aspects of cultural genocide involve a wide variety of social changes that have been imposed on Indian nations with disruptive

Stiffarm and Phil Lane, Jr., "The Demography of Native North America: A Question of American Indian Survival," in *The State of Native America: Genocide, Colonization, and Resistance*, ed. M. Annette Jaimes (Boston: South End Press, 1992), 23–53.

7. The latter distinguishes cultural genocide, as I have defined it, from situations like that currently prevailing between Russia and Lithuania. For Lithuania, political viability much more than cultural viability is at stake. Perhaps some Wittgensteinian notion of family resemblance categorization needs to be worked out here to distinguish the sufficient cultural disparateness necessary to threaten the cultural viability of a weaker entity.

8. White reformers during the post–Civil War era, the so-called "friends of the Indian," commonly charged that the United States had failed to fulfill the obligations of a single treaty signed with Indian people. Whipple, *Lights and Shadows of a Long Episcopate*, and Helen Hunt Jackson, *A Century of Dishonor: A Sketch of the United States Government's Dealing with Some of the Indian Tribes* (New York: 1881), are two prominent white spokespeople of that era who acknowledge this fact. Whipple repeats the allegation in his introduction to Jackson's volume.

9. On the Civilization Act (1819), see Francis Paul Prucha, *American Indian Policy in the Formative Years: The Indian Trade and Intercourse Acts, 1790–1834* (Cambridge: Harvard Univ. Press, 1962); and Bernard Sheehan, *Seeds of Extinctcion: Jeffersonian Philanthropy and the American Indian* (New York: W. W. Norton, 1974).

10. For a discussion of the Indian reform movement and the resulting "Peace Policy"

of the Grant administration, see Robert Winston Mardock, *The Reformers and the American Indian* (Columbia: Univ. of Missouri Press, 1971); Francis Paul Prucha, *American Indian Policy in Crisis: Christian Reformers and the Indian, 1865–1900* (Norman: Univ. of Oklahoma Press, 1976); and Henry E. Fritz, *The Movement for Indian Assimilation, 1860* (Westport, Conn.: Greenwood Press, 1981).

11. For a detailed description of the uneasy but collusive relationship between the Mormon Church and the U.S. government in dealing with the native inhabitants of Utah, see Gustive O. Larson, "Brigham Young and the Indians," in *The American West: An Appraisal*, ed. Robert G. Ferris (Santa Fe: Museum of New Mexico, 1963), 176–87. See also Francis Paul Prucha, *The Great Father: The United States Government and the American Indians*, 2 vols. (Lincoln: Univ. of Nebraska Press, 1984), 1:374–80.

12. Antonia Fabié, *Vida y escritos de Don Fray Bartolomé de Las Casas* (Madrid, 1879), 2:83ff.; English translation in Benno M. Biermann, "Bartolomé de Las Casas and Verapaz," in *Bartolomé De Las Casas in History: Toward an Understanding of the Man and His Work*, ed. Juan Friede and Benjamin Keen (De Kalb: Univ. of Northern Illinois Press, 1971), 453.

13. For the establishment of the reservation policy, see Prucha, *The Great Father*, "Part Three: American Expansion and the Reservation System," 1:315–410; and Edmund Jefferson Danziger, Jr., *Indians and Bureaucrats: Administering the Reservation Policy during the Civil War* (Champaign: Univ. of Illinois Press, 1974).

14. Dee Brown, *Bury My Heart at Wounded Knee* (New York: Holt, Rinehart and Winston, 1970), 13_36.

15. See Richard Erdoes, *The*

consequences. These include seemingly minor changes in personal behavior as well as changes that are fundamental to group cohesion. The latter may be obvious attacks on the relationships that bind a community together, such as the missionary proclivity for imposing the nuclear family ideal and displacing the extended kinship system upon which an Indian nation and individuals depend for their identity. The former can be just as dislocative. When conversion to the gospel of Jesus Christ is measured by the length of one's hair, cutting a man's hair is more than a symbolic change in personal behavior. It immediately changes his status within the group. Indeed, it effectively separates him from the group and generates a fundamental social shift from the independence of a healthy interdependent community to a dysfunctional codependent relationship between an alienated remnant of a conquered people and their conquerors.

The Ideology of White Superiority and Cultural Genocide

The missionaries were people of their own times and especially of their own cultural heritage. As a result, they came to Indian country with a particular frame of reference for understanding the Indian context and formed notions for the solution of Indian problems out of their own European cultural perception of the world. Because of their own cultural self-understanding, the missionaries, like the U.S. government, did not hesitate to impose their solutions or their culture on Indian people. The prevailing and thoroughly entrenched philosophical presupposition that fueled all European attitudes toward Indians was one of pronounced cultural and intellectual superiority.[18] The notion of European superiority over native peoples goes back to the very beginnings of the European invasion, as Columbus's own diary entry for October 12, 1492, documents. His immediate reaction to his first encounter with western hemisphere peoples included thoughts of domination and enslavement:

> [October 12, 1492] They ought to make good and skilled servants, for they repeat very quickly whatever we say to them. I think they can easily be made Christians, for they seem to have no religion. If it pleases Our Lord, I will take six of them to Your Highnesses when I depart. . . .[October 14] . . . these people are very unskilled in arms. Your Highnesses will see this for yourselves when I bring to you the seven that I have taken. After they learn our language I shall return them, unless Your Highnesses order that the entire population be taken to Castile, or held captive here. With 50 men you could subject everyone and make them do what you wished.[19]

This European/Euroamerican notion of superiority works its way out in at least two general branches of a historical trajectory—a trajectory that used inherent superiority as a rationalization for conquest and even genocide. It became a justification for slavery and the *encomienda* system among Spanish immigrants and, later, an excuse for punishing the "hostiles" in the western United States in order to tame their perceived savagery. The other branch of the same trajectory led to a much more sympathetic concern for "the Indians," but one that saw the resolution of "the Indian problem" in the replacement of Indian culture with European culture, sometimes blatantly referred to as "Christian culture" or "Christian civilization."[20] It was this second branch of the trajectory that energized the missionary endeavor, but around an arrogance that never questioned its clear goal of Christianizing and civilizing the savages, whom Whipple called "wild Indians."[21]

My point is not just to chastise the missionaries. Not only would that serve little purpose, but it would be asking these forebears in the faith to have done the impossible—namely, to have demonstrated an awareness beyond what was culturally possible at that time. Instead, my investigation has a primary objective and two closely related subordinate objectives. First, this analysis is part of an ongoing process of owning our history, honestly knowing our past, so that our future may be freed from living in a cover-up mode and our decisions for the future may be most creative and life-giving. It is equally crucial for white Americans to recognize occasions of oppressing others in their past and for Native American peoples to identify the sources of the oppression they have experienced and continue to experience.

Modern writers continue to expose the past and present oppression and exploitation of Native Americans in ways that call into question the whole process of modern political systems.[22] Yet the churches have somehow avoided recognition of their participation in this history of destruction and oppression.

My second objective is to provide a better understanding of what is at stake in the evangelization process. If we concede good intentions to the missionaries in general, we also must be careful to recognize them as people of their own times, incapable of the hindsight of critical analysis with which we are more likely to be blessed. That they confused their spiritual proclamation of the gospel of Jesus Christ with the imposition of new and strange cultural models for daily life is today inexcusable. But a century and more ago, the distinction between gospel and Euroamerican culture was far less clear. Add to that the apparent cultural superiority, in the European mind at least, of wearing clothes, using a fork, and other seeming technological wonders. Moreover, the missionaries most often came to an Indian nation after the effects of conquest had already become visible, increasing the missionaries' sense of their own cultural superiority. . . .

Good Intentions, Naïveté, and Genocide

At one level at least, I have presumed a certain naïveté with respect to the complicity of the missionaries in acts of cultural genocide. They surely did not intend any harm to Indian people, yet their blindness to their own inculturation of European values and social structures meant that complicity was unavoidable. That is, even at this initial level of analysis, it is clear that the missionaries were myopic regarding their own cultural biases. They engaged in actions that were a genuinely naïve imposition of their own cultural values and models of society on tribal peoples for whom the experience became dislocative and disruptive. The goals of the missionaries emerged out of a reservoir of what Wittgenstein called "common sense knowledge." They could reflect on that knowledge only within the limitations of their contemporary cultural self-awareness. The parameters of the world are defined by the subjective perception of the individual and the cultural community of individuals who tend to communicate easily with one another and agree generally about the interpretation of their experiences. The missionaries all came to Native American tribal communities

Sun Dance People: The Plains Indians, Past and Present (New York: Vintage, 1972), 175; and Vine Deloria, Jr., *Indians of the Pacific Northwest: From the Coming of the White Man to the Present Day* (Garden City, N.Y.: Doubleday, 1977), 9ff.

16. Brown, *Bury My Heart at Wounded Knee*, 414–45. For a contemporary account by an anthropologist, see James Mooney, *The Ghost-Dance Religion and the Sioux Outbreak of 1890* (Washington, D.C.: Bureau of American Ethnology, 1896). Nicholas Black Elk gives a Lakota eyewitness account, recorded in *Black Elk Speaks*, ed. John Neihardt (New York: Morrow, 1932); and a fine modern political analysis can be found in Ward Churchill, "The Earth Is Our Mother," in *The State of Native America*, 139–88.

17. Canadian history is likewise filled with examples of cultural genocide. The Canadian "Indian Act" of 1927 outlawed the potlatch ceremony, which has both social and religious aspects: Every Indian or other person who engages in, or assists in celebrating or encourages either directly or indirectly another to celebrate any Indian festival, dance or other ceremony of which the giving away or paying or giving back of money, goods or articles of any sort forms a part, or is a feature, whether such gift of money, goods or articles takes place before, at, or after the celebration of the same, or who engages or assists in any celebration or dance of which the wounding or mutilation of the dead or living body of any human being or animal forms a part or is a feature, is guilty of an offence and is liable on summary conviction to imprisonment for a term not exceeding six months and not less than two months. *Revised Statutes of Canada*, 1927: vol. 2, chap. 98, no. 140, p. 2218.

18. See Robert F. Berkhofer, Jr., *The White Man's Indian* (New York: Knopf, 1978); Gary B. Nash, *Red, White, and Black: The Peoples of Early America* (Englewood Cliffs, N.J.: Prentice-Hall, 1974); James Axtell, *The European and the Indian: Essays in the Ethnohistory of Colonial North America* (Oxford: Oxford Univ. Press, 1981); and Francis Jennings, *The Invasion of America: Indians, Colonialism and the Cant of Conquest* (New York: W. W. Norton, 1975).

19. Robert H. Fuson, ed. and trans., *The Log of Christopher Columbus* (Camden, Maine: International Marine Publishing Company, 1987), 77, 80.

20. See, for example, the publication of the Women's National Indian Association, with Baptist affiliation and a nondenominational, evangelical stance: *Christian Civilization and Missionary Work of the Women's National Indian Association* (Philadelphia, 1887). Quite aside from the implications connoted by the phrases "Christian civilization" and "Christian culture," one might wonder how this might be compared with a Muslim or Buddhist civilization or culture.

21. Jennings, *The Invasion of America*, especially chap. 1, "Crusader Ideology," 3–14. See also Bernard W. Sheehan, *Savagism and Civility: Indians and Englishmen in Colonial Virginia* (New York: Cambridge Univ. Press, 1980), especially chap. 2, "Conversion."

22. For example, see Ward Churchill and Jim Vander Wall, *Agents of Repression: The FBI's Secret Wars against the Black Panther Party and the American Indian Movement* (Boston: South End Press, 1988); and Rex Weyler, *The Blood of the Land: The Government and Corporate War against the American Indian Movement* (New York: Vintage, 1984).

with firmly established commitments to their own European or Euroamerican cultures with their social structures and institutions. As a result, they naturally assumed the superiority of the institutions and social structures of their own world and readily imposed them on Indian people. At the bottom line, then, this cultural myopia of the missionaries functioned to facilitate the exploitation of Indian people by both the government and the private sector or by the land-hungry immigrant farmers encroaching ever further onto the plains. Identifying their actions as well-intentioned but misguided certainly does not exonerate the missionaries. It merely serves to explain behavior that is finally inconsistent with the goal of salvation they proclaimed, and as responsible human beings they must be held accountable for the disastrous consequences of their actions.

At this level of analysis, the failure of the missionaries must be understood not just in individual terms but as systemic failure. The culpability of the individual missionaries for imposing their culture on Native Americans and perpetuating the lie of white superiority was in actuality prescribed from the outset by European and Euroamerican social structures. That is to say, it was impossible for any missionary to avoid complicity in the genocide of Native American peoples. Again in this case, recognizing the broader, structural impetus of Western social structures toward the assertion of white hegemony dare not become an excuse for exonerating the individual's participation in the dysfunctionality of the whole. Nevertheless, this recognition does push beyond the criticism of individual missionaries to an analysis of the systemic. This, in turn, raises two questions. First, what aspects of Western, Euroamerican culture have historically generated such myopic social and theological arrogance? Second, if the missionaries, with the best of intentions, perpetrated such havoc among Indian peoples, what does our own, modern myopia conceal from us, whatever our intentions to the contrary?

Finally, at a certain level of analysis, the presumed naïveté of the missionaries begins to fade as a justification for their behavior, and it becomes far more difficult to protect their memory even minimally by appealing to the spirit of the times or the pervasiveness of attitudes among Euroamerican peoples. How could these dedicated spiritual figures not see the role they inevitably played in the economic exploitation or the political manipulation of the tribal peoples of North America? More devastating to Indian communities than the imposition of new cultural standards was the missionaries' tendency to act consistently, sometimes self-consciously and sometimes implicitly, in the best interests of the economic and political structures of their Western cultural world. Thus, it was almost natural for the missionaries to participate in the political process of subjugation and to support the repressive efforts of their own government in whatever program had been devised at the time to serve that interest. It was just as natural for them to support the economic enterprises that manipulated and exploited Indian labor and resources. What finally must be realized is that the missionaries were deeply involved in symbiotic relationships with the very structures of power that crushed Indian resistance to the European invasion every step of the way, as Manifest Destiny moved "From California to the New York Island, from the redwood forest to the gulf stream waters."

Katie Geneva Cannon's gripping essay examines American slave history through the prism of her own African American ancestors. It first appeared in the book, Inheriting Our Mothers' Gardens: Feminist Theology in Third World Perspective. *Dr. Cannon is Associate Professor of Religion at Temple University, Philadelphia, and an ordained minister in the Presbyterian Church (U.S.A.).*

I am most aware of the rich lore I inherited from my mother's garden in Kannapolis, North Carolina. I recall particularly the stories shared during devastating thunderstorms. Whenever there were gusty winds and heavy rain accompanied by lightning and thunder, the Cannon household became—and still becomes—a folklore sanctuary. We turn off all the lights, unplug electrical appliances, and leave the supper dishes sitting in the kitchen sink. When the whole family is seated strategically around the kerosene lantern, my mother, Corine Lytle Cannon, moves into her role as creative storyteller.[1]

My mother's style is to reminisce around a stock of historical images, themes, and cultural expressions that tell the story of the origin of Black people in America. Much of what she recounts is based on testimony shared across generations that her father, Emmanuel Clayton Lytle, born August 21, 1865, was the only free child in his family. My grandfather's parents, siblings, and all others who preceded him were born into slavery. One of our favorite family legends centers around his mother, my maternal great-grandmother, Mary Nancy Lytle, born in 1832. When freedom finally came, Grandma Mary walked hundreds of miles, from plantation to plantation, looking for the children who had been taken from her and sold as slaves. With only instinct to guide her, Grandma Mary persisted until she found all her children and brought the family back together.

As direct descendants of African-American slaves, my family understands such tales as the indispensable source of Black people's historical confidence and spiritual persistence despite all oppression. My mother's keen memory and her extraordinary artistic sense enable her to pass on eyewitness accounts from freed relatives to succeeding generations. These narratives are the soil where my inheritance from my mother's garden grew.

Historical Context

As a student of slave narratives, seeking the interior garden of Afro-American culture, I discovered unmistakable evidence that racial slavery in the United States was the cruelest of institutions. The unmitigated severity of slavery was based on the assumed principle of human chattelhood. As early as 1660, it was decreed that henceforth all Africans—and only Africans and their descendants—entering the Colonies would be subjected to an entire institutional framework that required them to be treated as objects, as possessions, rather than as human beings. The principle of chattelhood enabled the inner dynamics of racial slavery to expand until it penetrated the basic institutional and ideological underpinnings of the entire normative order of society.

Acquisition of Slaves

The "middle passage," the transoceanic travel of captive and enslaved Africans, has been described as the most traumatizing mass human migration in modern history. Over a period of nearly four centuries, somewhere between 9 million and 50 million people from central and western areas of Africa were seized, loaded on ships and transported to the Americas. Each year slavers systematically hunted tens of thousands of African women, men, and children, chained them in coffles, and packed them in barracoons. People of different tribes, languages, and cultures were driven along in caravans, placed in the dungeons of slave castles or corral-like stock pens, and branded with the slave company's mark. Then they were shackled and crammed into the poorly ventilated holds of small ships, with their faces pressed against the backs of those lying in front of them. The treatment was so harsh that one out of every eight Africans died en route. So much wretchedness was never condensed in so little room as in the slave ships.

Status of Slaves

The status of chattel—mere property—was permanent, hereditary, and strictly racial. African and African American women, men, and children were reduced to the condition of livestock and their value was calculated in real estate terms. Of all western slaveholding areas, it was in the United States that slaves were defined most completely as sources of capital accumulation and commodities. All Afro-Americans (Blacks) were presumed to be slaves unless they could establish that they had been legally freed. The legalization of chattel slavery meant that the overwhelming majority of Blacks lived permanently in subhuman status. No objective circumstance—education, skill, dress, or bearing—could modify this fundamentally racist arrangement. This mode of racial domination meant that as chattel slaves none of my ancestors were human beings legally, culturally, socially, or politically. They had no socially recognized personhood. Their status in U.S. society was literally as things. The institution of slavery and its corollaries, white supremacy and racial bigotry, excluded Black people from every normal human consideration.

Afro-Americans faced many assaults, both cultural and physical. Like domestic animals, they were literally called "stock." Their children were anticipated as "increase." My Black foremothers were referred to as "brood sows and breeders." My Black forefathers, when sold, were described, as were horses, as either "sound or unsound." At slave auctions, Black people were stripped naked, exposed to public view, and dehumanized with pokes, probes, and crude physical examinations. Often, traders made slaves run, leap, and perform acts of agility to demonstrate their "value" as chattel.

Contemporary assessments of racial slavery cannot afford to ignore this history of the virtually unlimited power of white slaveholders. The submission required of slaves was unbounded. Armed with absolute dominion over the slave, the master's power extended to every dimension, including life and death. Slaveholders had the power to kill slaves with impunity. If a slave was injured or killed by someone else, the master could claim compensation comparable to damages due when an animal was harmed. A slave suffering from such a wrong was not considered the injured party. The slaveholder was considered to be the sufferer, damaged because of the loss of the slave's labor. The death of a slave required neither official investigation nor report, any more than did the death of cattle. Non-Blacks on the American scene portrayed Black slaves to be dumb, stupid, or contented, capable of doglike devotion, wanting in basic human qualities. They used such caricatures to convince themselves that the human beings whom they violated, degraded, and humiliated or whose well-being they did not protect were unworthy of anything better.

Conditions of Slavery

Classified as pieces of movable property, devoid of the minimum human rights society conferred on others, my great-grandparents could neither own property nor make contracts. As slaves, they were not permitted to buy or sell anything at all except as their masters' agents. They could not give or receive gifts. They could not travel without a pass. Afro-Americans had no security and no protection against insults and deliberate injuries inflicted on them. There was no one to hear their complaints of ill-treatment, no power of appeal, no redress whatever. In essence, Black women, men, and children were denied all the conventionalized prerogatives of the human condition defined by the American culture.

Forced into the precise and irrevocable category of perpetual servitude *durante vita*, for all generations, Black people could not be legally married. Without the legal status of marriage, the union of a female slave and a male slave was considered as "cohabitation," which was tolerated but might be terminated at will by slaveholders. White people differentiated between the basic rights and patterns of the family life they claimed for themselves as a "democratic" nation and those they deemed just treatment for their human merchandise.

One former slave recalled:

> My pa b'longin' to one man and my mammy b'longin' to another, four or five miles apart, caused some confusion, mix-up, and heartaches. My pa have to git a pass to come to see my mammy. He come sometimes without de pass. Patrollers catch him way up de chimney hidin' one night; they stripped him right befo' mammy and give him thirty-nine lashes, wid her cryin' and a hollerin' louder than he did.[2]

Slaves were constantly being robbed of familiar social ties in order that slaveholders could maximize their profits. All of the slave's relationships existed under the shadowy but imminent threat of permanent separation. Black people lived in constant fear and regularly had to endure the reality of having their husbands, wives, and children sold away from them under conditions that made it unlikely that they would ever see one another again. Relationships between both blood kin and friends were broken up by the interstate migration of slave labor. Slaveholders were at liberty to give, sell, or bequeath African Americans to other persons.

> A slave owner who broke up a family was not heartless by his lights. The kindliest of masters saw nothing wrong in giving a slave child to his son or daughter when they married. An economically pressed planter might regret that husbands and wives would be separated if he moved to the Southwest, but what

could he do? Sometimes debts mounted and slaves were seized by the sheriff or owners died and estates were divided.[3]

Countless slave families were forcibly disrupted.

Exploitation of Slave Workers

Be it in the Piedmont section, tidewater Virginia, the rice districts of South Carolina, or the lower Mississippi Valley, stories abound concerning my ancestors' lot, memories of stripes and torture. Their labor was coerced without wages, extorted by brute force. Slaveholders inflicted on slaves any severity they deemed necessary to make slaves perform required tasks and meted out any sort or degree of punishment for failure to work as expected or for otherwise incurring their displeasure.

Answerable with their bodies for all offenses, slaves were beaten with horse whips, cow straps, and a variety of blunt weapons. They suffered from scaling, burning, rape, and castration, sometimes dying from such inflictions. The great cruelty exhibited toward slaves resulted in instances of gouged-out eyes, slit tongues, and dismembered limbs. Sometimes slaves were physically marked by brands or tattoos or by wooden yokes or iron collars with long extended spokes. The callous and brutal system of slavery required a considerable number of slaves to wear chains, not only in the field during working hours but also at night in their living quarters. Eli Coleman, born a slave in 1846, recalled:

> Massa whooped a slave if he got stubborn or lazy. He whooped one so hard that the slave said he'd kill him. So Massa done put a chain round his legs, so he jes' hardly walk, and he has to work in the fields that way. At night he put 'nother chain round his neck and fastened it to a tree.[4]

The stark fact is that even while slaves lived under differing degrees of harshness, all slaves served under continuous duress.

> A handsome mulatto woman, about 18 or 20 years of age, whose independent spirit could not brook the degradation of slavery, was in the habit of running away; for this offence she had been repeatedly sent by her master and mistress to be whipped by the keeper of the Charleston workhouse. This had been done with such inhuman severity, as to lacerate her back in a most shocking manner; a finger could not be laid between the cuts. But the love of liberty was too strong to be annihilated by torture; and as a last resort, she was whipped at several different times, and kept a close prisoner. A heavy iron collar, with three prongs projecting from it, was placed around her neck, and a strong and sound front tooth was extracted to serve as a mark to describe her, in case of escape.[5]

The atrocious mutilation, too often practiced, was deeply rooted in and closely bound up with the whole existing system of chattelhood. The forms of permitted coercion effected a more complete dehumanization of slaves than had other institutional forms of slavery in earlier societies. Never before U.S. chattel slavery was a people so systematically deprived of their human rights and submerged in abject misery. The intent was to crush the spirit and will in order to transform an entire race of people, their lives and their labor, into basic commodities of production and re-production. White supremacists in the antebellum South believed that such systematic terrorism was absolutely necessary for the continuance of their highly prized way of life and of the economic organization, social relations, and political conditions necessary to it.

Even though the customary methods of enslavement were harsh and even ferocious, Black people worked in every branch of colonial trade and commerce. In addition to the gang labor on cotton, rice, tobacco, and sugarcane plantations, Black women and men worked as cooks, waiters, nurses, carpenters, masons, valets, gardeners, weavers, shoemakers, lumberjacks, and stevedores. Enslaved workers were also forced to work in mines, extracting coal, lead, iron, and gold. They built canals and pulled barges. Slaves dug tunnels, laid rails, and staffed the railroad system. Relegated to the quarries, slaves drilled and tapped explosives, cut and polished stones, and freighted them away. Working under the lash and guarded by overseers, bondswomen regularly performed virtually the same tasks as men.

The rigor of bondage meant that chattel slaves worked always at the discretion of their owners. They could not sell their own labor. My forebears had no say as to where, for whom, or how they would work. Slaveholders dictated the nature of the work, the times for labor and rest, and the amount of work to be performed. The fruit of Black labor could not convert to financial and material gains for Black people and their families. Black people were exploited both for white people's profit and their pleasure.

Hovering over all my cultural inheritance is the devastating reality that chattel tenure excluded any sort of social recognition of Black people as thinking, religious, and moral beings. My ancestors were forbidden by stringent laws to acquire an education or obtain the means to buy their own freedom. The dominant legal and social attitude was that slaves were to be kept ignorant and living a marginal existence, fed or famished, clothed or left naked, sheltered or unsheltered as served the slaveholder. In North Carolina it was a crime to distribute any pamphlet or book, including the Bible, among slaves. Only under rigidly specified conditions could Black people take part in services of worship. Preaching the gospel, assembling together, and learning to read and write were understood simply as obstacles to the maximization of slave identity. Black people were the only people in the United States ever explicitly forbidden by law to become literate.

Cultural Inheritance

Despite the devastations of slavery, with its unremitting exercise of raw planter power and unconstrained coercion, my ancestors had the hours from nightfall to daybreak to foster, sustain, and transmit cultural mechanisms that enabled them to cope with such bondage. In spite of every form of institutional constraint, Afro-American slaves were able to create another world, a counterculture within the white-defined world, complete with their own folklore, spirituals, and religious practices. These tales, songs, and prayers are the most distinctive cultural windows through which I was taught to see the nature and range of Black people's response to the dehumanizing pressures of slavery and plantation life. Even with cultural self-expression outlawed, my ancestors never surrendered their humanity or lost sight of a vision of freedom and justice they believed to be their due. There was a critical difference between what whites tried to teach and what slaves actually learned. Against all odds, Afro-American slaves created a culture saturated with their own values and heavily laden with their dreams.

Folklore

The folktales I have heard all my life were created by the slaves through-out the antebellum South as a strategy for coping with oppression and for turning their world upside down. Operating beneath a veil of pseudo-complacency, Black women and men tapped into a profound sense of cultural cohesion, creating an expressive system of coded messages to communicate what they considered good, worthy, and meaningful. Since their survival depended on keeping their true feelings undetected in the presence of whites, Afro-Americans employed the wit, intelligence, and ingenuity of Buh Fox, Buh Rabbit, the Squinch Owl, and others to over-whelm and defeat the powerful foes, Ole Massa and his wife. An ancient Black verse describes the pro-active phenomenon of folktales in this way:

> Got one mind for white folks to see
> Nother for what I know is me:
> He don't know, he don't know my mind.[6]

Many of the slave stories have a defensive verbal dimension so esoteric that white people miss their meanings altogether. Langston Hughes and Arna Bontemps elaborate this point in the following manner:

> While masters of slaves went to some length to get rid of tribal languages and some tribal customs, like certain practices of sor-cery, they accepted the animal stories as a harmless way to ease time or entertain the master's children. That the folk tales of these Negro slaves were actually projections of personal experi-ences and hopes and defeats in terms of symbols appears to have gone unnoticed.[7]

Scores and scores of Blacks projected their everyday experiences and their own sensibilities onto legendary figures like High John de Con-queror, John the Trickster, and Efram as a challenge to the slave system. As C. Eric Lincoln has written:

> Every black community in the South has its multitudes of leg-ends illustrating blacks' superior strength, sexual prowess, and moral integrity. "Mr. Charlie" is never a match for the cunning of "Ol' John." And "Miss Ann," though she is "as good a ol' white woman" as can be found anywhere, remains in the mind of the black southerner a white woman, and therefore a legiti-mate target for the machinations of her black servant, "Annie Mae."[8]

Living in a dialectical relationship with white supremacy, folklore was the essential medium by which the themes of freedom, resistance, and self-determination were evoked, preserved, and passed by word of mouth from generation to generation. Older slaves used folktales to reveal to their fellow slaves what they knew. As tradition bearers, they distilled this compendium of folk wisdom into instructional materials to teach younger slaves how to survive. The reappropriation of their own experiences afforded the slaves opportunities to strip away the social absurdity of chattelhood so carefully camouflaged in the dominant culture. In other words, folklore was the mask the slaves wore in order to indict slavery and to question the society in which it flourished. By objectifying their lives in folktales, Afro-American slaves were able to assert the dignity of their own persona and the invincibility of their cause.

Spirituals

Like many raconteurs, my mother always includes music in her storytelling sessions. While waiting for the ongoing storm to subside, my mother invites the family to join her in singing Afro-American spirituals. Beating time with our hands or feet, we sing about Mary weeping, Martha mourning, Peter sinking, and Thomas doubting. This genre of Black sacred music is a vital part of my family's religious tradition.

The music we listen to and sing at home is in the tradition of my ancestors, musicians who fashioned their songs from biblical lore, traditional African tunes, Protestant hymns, and the crucible of their experiences under slavery. Using their own distinct phrases, improvisational structure, polyrhythms, and call-and-response patterns, Black women and men expressed their consciousness and identity as a religious people. Some of their songs were slow drawn-out "sorrow tunes" that reflected the mood of suffering in the midst of unspeakable cruelty.

Nobody knows de trubble I sees,
Nobody knows but Jesus,
Nobody knows de trubble I sees,
Glory hallelu!

Other spirituals were liturgical shouts and jubilees, songs with reference to a future happy time. These required upbeat tempos accompanied by rhythmic clapping and holy dancing.

Oh, my soul got happy
When I come out the wilderness,
Come out the wilderness,
Come out the wilderness,
Oh, my soul got happy
When I come out the wilderness,
I'm leanin' on the Lawd.

A number of spirituals were veiled protest songs used to announce secret meetings, planned escapes, and the route and risk of the freedom trail.

Steal away, steal away,
Steal away to Jesus!
Steal away, steal away home,
I ain't got long to stay here!

In essence, spirituals were the indispensable device that slaves, forbidden by slaveholders to worship or, in most cases, even to pray, used to transmit a worldview fundamentally different from and opposed to that of slaveholders. For instance, slaveholders spoke of slavery being "God ordained," while slaves sang

> O Freedom! O Freedom!
> O Freedom, I love thee!
> And before I be a slave,
> I'll be buried in my grave,
> And go home to my Lord and be free.

The spirituals express my ancestors' unflinching faith that they, too, were people of God.

As spiritual singers, slaves were not bothered by the chronological distance between the biblical era and their present. Operating on a sense of sacred time, they extended time backward so as to experience an immediate intimacy with biblical persons as faith relatives. In other words, the characters, scenes, and events from the Bible came dramatically alive in the midst of their estrangement. The trials and triumphs of Noah riding out the flood, Moses telling Pharaoh to let God's people go, Jacob wrestling all night with an angel, Daniel being delivered from the lion's den, Shadrach, Meshach and Abednego walking in the midst of flames, Joshua fighting the battle of Jericho, and Jesus praying in the Garden of Gethsemane are some of the Bible stories my foreparents committed to music as they interpreted their own experience against a wider narrative of hope and courage.

Prayer

When the rainfall's intensity and the wind's velocity drop and the lightning and the thunder recede, I know that the end of the storytelling is near. Believing that a direct personal relationship with God exists, my mother always concludes her stories with a long prayer of intercession, praise, and thanksgiving. Kneeling beside the couch, she prays for the needs of both the immediate and the extended family. She celebrates God's goodness, majesty, and mercy. She frequently enunciates thanks for the gifts of the earth and for all the blessings received. After a period of silence, my mother then provides time for every family member to bear witness to the immediate power of Jesus as "heart fixer and mind regulator."

This sacred corporate event is the direct and natural successor to the oral folklore and the religious music inherited from Afro-American slaves. Hence I grew up understanding the Black prayer tradition to be the authentic living bridge between Black people's stories, Black people's music, and Black people's source of faith.

In the past, my ancestors met in secluded places—woods, gullies, ravines, and thickets (aptly called "hush harbors")—to pray without being detected. Adeline Hedges, born a slave in Alabama, attests to the importance of prayer:

> De slaves warn't 'lowed to go to church, but dey would whisper roun, and all met in de woods and pray. De only time I 'members my pa was one time when I was a li'l chile, he set me on a log by him an' prayed.[9]

Sometimes they prayed while huddled behind wet quilts and rags that had been hung up on the form of a church or tabernacle, in order to

Endnotes

1. Victoria Byerly, *Hard Times Cotton Mill Girls: Personal Histories of Womanhood and Poverty in the South* (Ithaca, N.Y.: ILR Press, 1986), pp. 143–60.
2. Dorothy Sterling, ed., *We Are Your Sisters: Black Women in the Nineteenth Century* (New York: W. W. Norton & Co., 1984), pp. 42–43.
3. Ibid., p. 43.
4. George R. Rawick, *From Sundown to Sunup: The*

prevent their words from carrying through the air. Other times they formed a circle on their knees and spoke their words into and over a vessel of water to drown out the sound. Ellen Butler, born a slave in Louisiana in 1859, witnesses to this dimension of slave religion:

> Massa never 'lowed us slaves to go to church but they have big holes in the fields they gits down in and prays. They done that way 'cause the white folks didn't want them to pray. They used to pray for freedom.[10]

The tradition of the slaves' "hush harbor" prayer meetings lives on in my parents' home. With the abiding strength of the family legends planted in our hearts, my mother invites each one of us to pray, quote scripture, lead a song, or give a testimony. Speaking under the unction and guidance of the Holy Spirit, my father, Esau Cannon, testifies about his personal experience with God. My grandmother, Rosa Lytle, "lines out" in long-metered style her favorite psalms and spirituals. The rest of the family interjects Bible verses between the singing. The last thing we utter before retiring to bed is always Grandma Rosie's prayer:

> And when waste and age
> and shock and strife
> shall have sapped
> these walls of life,
> Then take this dust
> that's earthly worn
> and mold it
> into heavenly form.

Such is my inheritance.

Making of the Black Community (Westport, Conn.: Greenwood Publishing Co., 1972), p. 57.
5. Testimony of Sarah M. Grimké, abolitionist from South Carolina, in [Theodore D. Weld], *American Slavery As It Is: Testimony of a Thousand Witnesses* (American Anti-Slavery Society, 1839), cited in Gerda Lerner, ed., *Black Women in White America: A Documentary History* (New York: Vintage Books, 1972), p. 18.
6. Cited by Robert E. Hemenway in the Introduction to *Mules and Men*, by Zora Neale Hurston (Bloomington, Ind.: Indiana University Press, 1978), p. xxi.
7. Langston Hughes and Arna Bontemps, ed., *The Book of Negro Folklore* (New York: Dodd, Mead & Co., 1958), p. viii.
8. C. Eric Lincoln, *The Black Muslims in America* (Boston: Beacon Press, 1973), p. 35.
9. Rawick, p. 35.
10. Ibid.

Richard Rodriguez

Richard Rodriguez provides vivid glimpses into the life and thinking of his parents—Mexican immigrants to California; and into his own childhood experience with English as a foreign language. These passages come from his haunting "intellectual autobiography," **Hunger of Memory: The Education of Richard Rodriguez.** *Mr. Rodriguez is an editor at* Pacific News Service *and writes regularly for the* **Los Angeles Sunday Times.**

I was a bilingual child, a certain kind—socially disadvantaged—the son of working-class parents, both Mexican immigrants.

In the early years of my boyhood, my parents coped very well in America. My father had steady work. My mother managed at home. They were nobody's victims. Optimism and ambition led them to a house (our home) many blocks from the Mexican south side of town. We lived among *gringos* and only a block from the biggest, whitest houses. It never occurred to my parents that they couldn't live wherever they chose. Nor was the Sacramento of the fifties bent on teaching them a contrary lesson. My mother and father were more annoyed than intimidated by those two or three neighbors who tried initially to make us unwelcome. ("Keep your brats away from my sidewalk!") But despite all they achieved, perhaps because they had so much to achieve, any deep feeling of ease, the confidence of "belonging" in public was withheld from them both. They regarded the people at work, the faces in crowds, as very distant from us. They were the others, *los gringos*. That term was interchangeable in their speech with another, even more telling, *los americanos*.

I grew up in a house where the only regular guests were my relations. For one day, enormous families of relatives would visit and there would be so many people that the noise and the bodies would spill out to the backyard and front porch. Then, for weeks, no one came by. (It was usually a salesman who rang the doorbell.) Our house stood apart. A gaudy yellow in a row of white bungalows. We were the people with the noisy dog. The peoplo raised pigeons and chickens. We were the foreigners on the block. A few neighbors smiled and waved. We waved back. But no one in the family knew the names of the old couple who lived next door; until I was seven years old, I did not know the names of the kids who lived across the street.

In public, my father and mother spoke a hesitant, accented, not always grammatical English. And they would have to strain—their bodies tense—to catch the sense of what was rapidly said by *los gringos*. At home they spoke Spanish. The language of their Mexican past sounded in counterpoint to the English of public society. The words would come quickly, with ease. Conveyed through those sounds was the pleasing, soothing, consoling reminder of being at home.

During those years when I was first conscious of hearing, my mother and father addressed me only in Spanish; in Spanish I learned to reply. By contrast, English (*inglés*), rarely heard in the house, was the language I came to associate with *gringos*. I learned my first words of English overhearing my parents speak to strangers. At five years of age, I knew just enough English for my mother to trust me on errands to stores one block away. No more.

I was a listening child, careful to hear the very different sounds of Spanish and English. Wide-eyed with hearing, I'd listen to sounds more than words. First, there were English (*gringo*) sounds. So many words were still unknown that when the butcher or the lady at the drugstore said something to me, exotic polysyllabic sounds would bloom in the midst of their sentences. Often, the speech of people in public seemed to me very loud, booming with confidence. The man behind the counter would literally ask, "What can I do for you?" But by being so firm and so clear, the sound of his voice said that he was a *gringo*; he belonged in public society.

I would also hear then the high nasal notes of middle-class American speech. The air stirred with sound. Sometimes, even now, when I have been traveling abroad for several weeks, I will hear what I heard as a boy. In hotel lobbies or airports, in Turkey or Brazil, some Americans will pass, and suddenly I will hear it again—the high sound of American voices. For a few seconds I will hear it with pleasure, for it is now the sound of *my* society—a reminder of home. But inevitably—already on the flight headed for home—the sound fades with repetition. I will be unable to hear it anymore.

When I was a boy, things were different. The accent of *los gringos* was never pleasing nor was it hard to hear. Crowds at Safeway or at bus stops would be noisy with sound. And I would be forced to edge away from the chirping chatter above me.

I was unable to hear my own sounds, but I knew very well that I spoke English poorly. My words could not stretch far enough to form complete thoughts. And the words I did speak I didn't know well enough to make into distinct sounds. (Listeners would usually lower their heads, better to hear what I was trying to say.) It was more troubling for me to hear my parents speak in public: their high-whining vowels and gutteral consonants; their sentences that got stuck with 'eh' and 'ah' sounds; the confused syntax; the hesitant rhythm of sounds so different from the way *gringos* spoke. I'd notice, moreover, that my parents' voices were softer than those of *gringos* we'd meet.

I am tempted now to say that none of this mattered. In adulthood I am embarrassed by childhood fears. And, in a way, it didn't matter very much that my parents could not speak English with ease. Their linguistic difficulties had no serious consequences. My mother and father made themselves understood at the county hospital clinic and at government offices. And yet, in another way, it mattered very much—it was unsettling to hear my parents struggle with English. Hearing them, I'd grow nervous, my clutching trust in their protection and power weakened.

There were many times like the night at a brightly lit gasoline station (a blaring white memory) when I stood uneasily, hearing my father. He was talking to a teenaged attendant. I do not recall what they were saying, but I cannot forget the sounds my father made as he spoke. A one point his words slid together to form one word—sounds as confused as the threads of blue and green oil in the puddle next to my shoes. His voice rushed through what he had left to say. And, toward the end, reached falsetto notes, appealing to his listener's understanding. I looked away to the lights of passing automobiles. I tried not to hear anymore. But I heard only too well the calm, easy tones in the attendant's reply. Shortly afterward, walking toward home with my father, I shivered when he put his hand on my shoulder. The very first chance that I got, I evaded his grasp and ran on ahead into the dark, skipping with feigned boyish exuberance.

But then there was Spanish. *Español*: my family's language. *Español*: the language that seemed to me a private language. I'd hear strangers on the radio and in the Mexican Catholic church across town speaking in Spanish, but I couldn't really believe that Spanish was a public language, like English. Spanish speakers, rather, seemed related to me, for I sensed that we shared—through our language—the experience of feeling apart from *los gringos*. It was thus a ghetto Spanish that I heard and I spoke. Like those whose lives are bound by a barrio, I was reminded by Spanish of my separateness from *los otros, los gringos* in power. But more intensely than for most barrio children—because I did not live in a barrio—Spanish seemed to me the language of home. (Most days it was only at home that I'd hear it.) It became the language of joyful return.

A family member would say something to me and I would feel myself specially recognized. My parents would say something to me and I would feel embraced by the sounds of their words. Those sounds said: *I am speaking with ease in Spanish. I am addressing you in words I never use with* los gringos. *I recognize you as someone special, close, like no one outside. You belong with us. In the family.*

(Ricardo.)

At the age of five, six, well past the time when most other children no longer easily notice the difference between sounds uttered at home and words spoken in public, I had a different experience. I lived in a world magically compounded of sounds. I remained a child longer than most; I lingered too long, poised at the edge of language—often frightened by the sounds of *los gringos*, delighted by the sounds of Spanish at home. I shared with my family a language that was startlingly different from that used in the great city around us.

For me there were none of the gradations between public and private society so normal to a maturing child. Outside the house was public society; inside the house was private. Just opening or closing the screen door behind me was an important experience. I'd rarely leave home all alone or without reluctance. Walking down the sidewalk, under the canopy of tall trees, I'd warily notice the—suddenly—silent neighborhood kids who stood warily watching me. Nervously, I'd arrive at the grocery store to hear there the sounds of the *gringo*—foreign to me—reminding me that in this world so big, I was a foreigner. But then I'd return. Walking back toward our house, climbing the steps from the sidewalk, when the front door was open in summer, I'd hear voices beyond the screen door talking in Spanish. For a second or two, I'd stay, linger there, listening. Smililng, I'd hear my mother call out, saying in Spanish (words): 'Is that you, Richard?' All the while her sounds would assure me: *You are home now; come closer; inside. With us.*

"*Sí,*" I'd reply.

Once more inside the house I would resume (assume) my place in the family. The sounds would dim, grow harder to hear. Once more at home, I would grow less aware of that fact. It required, however, no more than the blurt of the doorbell to alert me to listen to sounds all over again. The house would turn instantly still while my mother went to the door. I'd hear her hard English sounds. I'd wait to hear her voice return to soft-sounding Spanish, which assured me, as surely as did the clicking tongue of the lock on the door, that the stranger was gone.

Plainly, it is not healthy to hear such sounds so often. It is not healthy to distinguish public words from private sounds so easily. I remained cloistered by sounds, timid and shy in public, too dependent on voices at home. And yet it needs to be emphasized: I was an extremely happy child at home. I remember many nights when my father would come back from work, and I'd hear him call out to my mother in Spanish, sounding relieved. In Spanish, he'd sound light and free notes he never could manage in English. Some nights I'd jump up just at hearing his voice. With *mis hermanos* I would come running into the room where he was with my mother. Our laughing (so deep was the pleasure!) became screaming. Like others who know the pain of public alienation, we transformed the knowledge of our public separateness and made it consoling—the reminder of intimacy. Excited, we joined our voices in a celebration of sounds. *We are speaking now the way we never speak out in public. We are alone—together*, voices sounded, surrounded to tell me. Some nights, no one seemed willing to loosen the hold sounds had on us. At dinner, we invented new words. (Ours sounded Spanish, but made sense only to us.) We pieced together new words by taking, say, an English verb and giving it Spanish endings. My mother's instructions at bedtime would be lacquered with mock-urgent tones. Or a word like *sí* would become, in several notes, able to convey added measures of feeling. Tongues explored the edges of words, especially the fat vowels. And we happily sounded that military drum roll, the twirling roar of the Spanish *r*. Family language: my family's sounds. The voices of my parents and sisters and brother. Their voices insisting: *You belong here. We are family members. Related. Special to one another. Listen!* Voices singing and sighing, rising, straining, then surging, teeming with pleasure that burst syllables into fragments of laughter. At times it seemed there was steady quiet only when, from another room, the rustling whispers of my parents faded and I moved closer to sleep.

&

Supporters of bilingual education today imply that students like me miss a great deal by not being taught in their family's language. What they seem not to recognize is that, as a socially disadvantaged child, I considered Spanish to be a private language. What I needed to learn in school was that I had the right—and the obligation—to speak the public language of *los gringos*. The odd truth is that my first-grade classmates could have become bilingual, in the conventional sense of that word, more easily than I. Had they been taught (as upper-middle-class children are often taught early) a second language like Spanish or French, they could have regarded it simply as that: another public language. In my case such bilingualism could not have been so quickly achieved. What I did not believe was that I could speak a single public language.

Without question, it would have pleased me to hear my teachers address me in Spanish when I entered the classroom. I would have felt much less afraid. I would have trusted them and responded with ease. But I would have delayed—for how long postponed?—having to learn the language of public society. I would have evaded—and for how long could I have afforded to delay?—learning the great lesson of school, that I had a public identity.

Mary Swander

Mary Swander, a fourth-generation Iowan, sketches two distinct kinds of European American experience within the culture of the United States: that of her Irish forebears and her own Irish Catholic childhood in the Midwest; and that of a fascinating group of religious outsiders in late-twentieth-century America, the Amish. This piece comes from her book, Out of This World: A Woman's Life Among the Amish. *Mary Swander is a poet and essayist. A regular commentator on Iowa Public Radio, she teaches creative writing at Iowa State University at Ames.*

I'm on my knees praying with the Beachy Amish congregation, facing the rear of the church, my lips moving, my folded hands resting on the pew seat. Beside me, Esther Chupp bows her head, her eyes closed. Throughout this service, I've taken my cue from Esther, squeezing into the seat beside her, with all the other women who take their position on the left side of the church, sharing her hymnal, my fingers supporting one side of the book, hers the other, my alto stabbing at the notes I sight-read, her soprano sliding up and down in familiarity. Though raised a Catholic, I've never quite gotten the hang of head bowing and eye lowering, so I stare straight ahead into the white prayer cap before me and take in the sleek, bare lines of this tiny church, its peaked roof and slanted ceiling, empty walls, its plain glass windows looking out onto the fall fields of corn and beans just waiting for the harvest.

Inside, the congregants' faces are as weathered as the church pews. The men, dressed in solid black trousers and lapel-less jackets that button high under their chins, showing just a flash of their white shirts near their faces, kneel on the right side of the church, shepherding their smaller sons close to their sides. Near the front of the church, the older children sit by themselves, boys on one side, girls on another. The girls, like their mothers, wear their hair long and swept up into buns at the back of their heads. The boys, like their fathers, wear theirs mid-ear in bowl cuts attended to at home by their mothers. The men's necks and faces are deeply tanned, their foreheads and ears a distinctly lighter shade from the protection of their summer straw hats. The women, with their younger daughters tucked close, are garbed in pastel dresses, white, pink, blue, and green, cut from the same pattern—puffed sleeves, pleated bodice, and full skirt. The minister stands at the front of the church on a raised platform. Nothing adorns this space but an oak podium where his Bible rests.

I have come to church with Esther as an act of friendship and solidarity, her gesture of welcoming me into the community, of declaring our bond in healing. I watch the stalks outside bend and sway in the morning breeze, thinking about my years of Catholicism, my knees imprinted with the lines of tongue-and-groove boards from hardwood floors, and realize what an odd thing I'm doing—kneeling in a Protestant church, this very strange deed probably a statement of dissent against my own religion.

❧

I am on my knees praying with the Manning, Iowa, Sacred Heart Church congregation, facing forward toward the huge cross that hangs over the altar, lips just beginning to recognize a few words of Latin—*Dominus vobiscum.* It is 1956 and I am six years old and wedged between my mother and grandmother on the left side of the church. Closer to the front, older children sit by themselves, boys on the right under the statue of Saint Joseph with his blossoming staff, girls on the left under the serene pose of the Blessed Virgin Mary. My hands are folded, pressing against the pew, fingers pointed straight ahead toward the Lord, the way I was taught in Catechism class, my right thumb draped on top of my left.

Over my shoulder, I wear a strap dangling a tiny white patent leather purse that holds a tiny white rosary and pipe cleaners. The adults around me keep their gazes fixed on the altar and beat their fists to their breasts at the ringing of the bells, but I slump back against the pew seat and take in, on one extreme, the Stations of the Cross carved from oak depicting the bloody Crucifixion, and on the other, the life-size statue of the Christ Child the women of the Holy Rosary Society have dressed in a long, flowing lace gown and golden crown.

Sun pours through the stained-glass windows, the deep red and blue rays brightening the flicker and glow of the rack of votive candles, casting a tint across the faces of the women in their pastel dresses, the men in their dark sports slacks and short-sleeved white shirts, collars open. An usher, his neck and arms tanned a deep brown, his brow and face ghostly white in comparison, reaches up with a pole to unlock and open one of the windows. It tilts toward me. Cooler air and a fly rush in, and I make out the lettering on the pane: In Loving Memory of Mr. and Mrs. Edward Signall . . . my great-grandparents.

My great-grandparents, who homesteaded near this small town of just 1,500 people in Carroll County, donated the land on which this ornate red brick church was built, and helped hammer together the small plain wooden structure that came before it. They also donated the plot for the Catholic cemetery, a piece of pasture they fenced off where they had buried their nine-year-old daughter, the youngest of their ten children. My grandmother, who drops her envelope into the basket at the offertory, is donating money for the construction of yet a third church, a sleek, new modern one that will look like a gas station. Our Lady of the Pumps.

My grandmother was the sacristan for the original edifice, opening up its doors and building a fire in its woodstove when a missionary priest happened to come to town to say Mass, washing and ironing the vestments and altar cloths, polishing the brass candle holders and chalice, mopping down the floors, and even painting the building outside and in before her own wedding. Now, she often still takes a turn at laundering the priest's chasuble, the long, flowing white garment with its golden cross embroidered across the back, flapping in the breeze from our clothesline on clear fall days.

I have been taken to church by my family as a member of our nuclear unit, as a part of our larger rural community, as an initiate into the mores and customs of our Irish tradition. We are here because this ritual of Sunday Mass feeds our need for a spiritual center in our lives. We are here because this ritual affirms our place in the order of things. It links us to other townspeople with similar values, beliefs, and heritage. It links us to other congregations in the diocese, throughout the state, the country, and the world.

We believe in one Catholic and apostolic church, we pray at the Confiteor. We believe in the universality of our religion, but we know that, on a smaller scale, it provided a memory of home for my immigrant great-grandparents, a piece of the old country, a social context to their lives. Even at six, I know that we often spend more time outside the church visiting with relatives and friends after Mass than we do inside praying. During the early settlement days on the prairie, when there were no phones or cars, when families lived in relative isolation during the week, the trip to town to church on Sunday was a crucial rite.

Edward Signall, my Episcopalian great-grandfather who converted the week before he died so he could be buried in the cemetery he donated, piled his wife and ten children into the buggy every Sunday morning, driving through mud, blizzards, and thunderstorms to make it to Mass on time. It was a sin *not* to go to Mass, but incentives abounded. Gossip was exchanged there, business deals cinched, marriages arranged. My family had a deep respect for the church, but also cautioned not to take it too seriously.

"Those priests and nuns." My grandmother used to roll her eyes while she fed vestments through the wringer of her washing machine. "Don't get too thick with them."

My grandfather, an old country doctor, used to rise and genuflect, leaving the church to be "available to his patients," at the end of Mass before the priest launched into what could be an interminable sermon. When the homily was moved to the beginning of the Mass, he kept the same habits, exiting every Sunday after a mere ten minutes in the pew.

Agnus Dei.

Even at six, I recognize the bond that religion creates. I do not yet understand the terrible gulf and hatred it can also engender. Secure but bored with my scenario this Sunday morning, my mind wanders to Saturday cartoons and cowboy shows. I take out my rosary and wrap it around my neck like a lasso. I fashion a pipe cleaner into a horse and pretend that I am Mary, queen of the heavenly Wild West, riding out through the gates of my celestial ranch.

❧

A horse gallops into the yard outside my grandparents' house in Perry, Iowa, a man in a long, flowing white gown carrying a torch. Other men, in white hoods, their eyes peering out of holes as in Halloween ghost costumes, erect a huge cross wrapped in straw, quickly pounding its point into the ground. It is near midnight, the fall sky dark, the air clear, a breeze blowing the rag my grandmother uses to clean the line still clothespinned to the rope. The man with the torch bends down and sets fire to the cross, flames bursting into the night.

"Papists. Foreigners," he yells.

It is 1920 and my mother is six. She is the first one awake, her bedroom window facing the front of the house in the attic of their stucco bungalow. She stares through the glass, her body shaking in her flannel nightgown. She hops out of bed, watching the backs of the heads of the hooded men charging down Main Street toward her father's office. He has been in practice but a few months, after having left Clifden, Ireland, marrying my grandmother and completing a residency in Chicago.

"Papa," she calls and dashes downstairs through the dark to her parents' bedroom, her bare feet cold on the hardwood floors. "Papa, Mama!"

My grandparents light a lamp, toss on their robes, and rush out onto the porch just in time to see the wink pick up a spark and carry it to the clothesline, where the rag catches on fire. "My God, they'll burn us out!" my grandfather bellows in his thick brogue, my grandmother already filling a bucket of water at the pump.

But soon the flames in the yard are doused, the rag stomped into the ground, the wooden cross nothing but a skeleton of ashes, and my grandmother scurries down the street to the office to check on its security, bucket in hand, as she does every morning at dawn to clean and mop down the examining rooms. Inside the house, my grandfather puts my mother on his knee, trying to ease her sobbing.

"Why did those men come and start a fire?" she cries, and he wraps his arms around her.

"They are hateful people."

"But why do they hate us?"

"We're Irish Catholics," he tries to explain.

"And they want to burn us up?"

"For hundreds of years certain groups of people have hated us."

"Why?"

"People learn to hate one another. But you must be strong—strong in your faith and yourself."

My grandparents stay in Perry only another year, just long enough for a Catholic medical practice in Atlantic, Iowa, to open up. Then they move father west and live within the shadow of Saint Peter and Paul's Church.

ॐ

Black-and-white snapshot number 1: I am nine, and we have moved to Davenport, all the way across Iowa to the easternmost border of the state, on the Mississippi River. I am dressed in white, my crinoline slip fluffing out the skirt of my Swiss polka dot dress, a garland of daisies in my hair, my patent leather purse slung over my shoulder, the pipe cleaners inside replaced by a small daily missal. I stand just outside Saint Paul's parish church, where minutes before I've made my First Communion. My hands are folded, my face peaceful but for the wrinkle of lines above my brows when I squint into the bright sun.

Snapshot number 2: Minutes later, tongue out, thumbs in my ears, hands waving fiercely at my tormentor, my face is scrunched into a grotesque scowl. One of my Protestant schoolmates from the public school has ridden by on his bicycle, jeering at me. He stops and pitches a rock in my direction. I pick it up and throw it back at him.

"Why are they throwing rocks at me?" I had sobbed in my mother's lap one day after school earlier that year.

I had gone to my new second grade, earned all A's on my report card, learned new jump rope chants, *Down the Mississippi, down the muddy Mississippi, where the boats go push,* become playmates with Bobbie, the Jewish neighbor girl down the street with the Stop and Go earmuffs, but never become integrated into the class. Head down, I worked hard in school, then walked home alone, for many of my classmates' mothers forbid them to play with me because of my religion. Then, throughout the spring of the year, I was dismissed three days a week, for two hours of special training in preparation for my First Communion. I rather enjoyed the sessions of instruction with the young priest, who laughed a lot and drew pictures of the Holy Trinity on the blackboard, but I dreaded leaving public school at ten in the morning, fishing my coat out of my locker and walking across the playground with taunts of "mackerel snapper" and the sting of small pebbles grazing my back.

"People learn to hate," my mother tries to explain.

"Why?"

"It's been going on for hundreds and hundreds of years. You must be strong in your faith and yourself."

The next day I walk home from school with Bobbie, tell her about the rock throwing, the talk with my mother. She tells me what her mother has told her about pogroms in Russia, about Nazi Germany and the Holocaust. My eyes widen and I stop still in the middle of the sidewalk.

ॐ

I am sitting on Moses and Miriam's porch swing, both feet dangling, my toes brushing the floorboards, back and forth, the seat squeaking *eeek, eeek,* creating its own rhythm and breeze. It is late September, the corn across the road crisp, drying to a golden light brown. I am thirty-nine years old and the temperature is sixty-nine degrees. Earlier, I had walked around the corner and knocked on Moses and Miriam's door for a visit. We decided to congregate outside, as the evening was so pleasant.

Now the leaves of the Norway maple tree in the yard rustle faintly with an almost inaudible stir, the sun setting, a purplish light spreading across the flat western horizon that stretches taut and secure as the twine wrapped across the bales of hay stacked in the barn. There, the stray cat has nestled in and delivered a litter of scrawny kittens in all colors— calico, fluffy white, solid gray, tiger stripes. A litter of cats can have several fathers, and this one looks like it's been fertilized by several denominations. In the morning, Miriam will cook oatmeal for these varied creatures, half of whom will die in a few weeks of distemper; Moses will carry the dish out to the barn, where the mother will slink up close, always alert, always suspicious, as any wild animal instinctively is, her nipples almost dragging on the ground, and lap at the cereal with her rough tongue.

One stray monarch butterfly drifts toward the windbreak of pines, and the gauzy outline of the full moon rises into the sky. A horse drawing a buggy ambles by, gravel clicking against wooden wheels, the battery-powered reflector blinking in the dark.

"Who's that going there?" Miriam asks, perched on the swing next to me in her nightgown and robe, her cheeks sunken into her face, a light chiffon scarf loosely draped over her gray hair, which falls down around her shoulders.

"Fannie," Moses says, flapping open the screen door with a huge bowl of popcorn he's fixed in the kitchen. "Sure, that's Fannie Yoder."

Fannie waves from the buggy, the horse slowing slightly.

"Fannie? That's not Fannie," Miriam says.

"Well, sure it is."

"Where's she going then so late at night?"

"I don't know. She didn't tell me," Moses jokes, scooping out popcorn from the larger bowl into smaller ones, handing one to his wife.

"I won't have any. Don't have my teeth in. But did you bring napkins?"

"Yes, I brought the napkins."

"Fannie? She's got church at her house tomorrow. You'd think she'd be at home getting ready."

"You go to church?" Moses turns to me.

I nod, not wanting to expound on my "recovering Catholic" status, the troubles I've had all my adult life reconciling many of the tenets of the church with my own convictions, the pull and tug I've felt between staying with and leaving an organization I've found at once stabilizing and repressive.

"Where do you go?"

"In Lakeland."

"Lakeland?" Moses swings around and stares me in the eye, knowing that there's only one church in that nearby town. "You're not a Catholic, are you?"

I nod again. "I was raised a Catholic."

Moses drops his hand into the popcorn bowl and Miriam stops still in the swing.

"Well," Moses says after several seconds' silence. "That's all right. That's all right too."

✌

The large white truck, "MENNONITE DISASTER SERVICE" stenciled on its side, is parked in the lot of Saint Joseph's Church. Life jacket, slicker, and knee-high rubber boots thrown into the back of my truck, I drive through a foot of water to find Mahlon and some of my other neighbors, Amish and Mennonite volunteers, who have come to Chelsea, Iowa, to help pump out basements in this flood-ravaged town. It is 1993, I'm forty-three, and this is the fifth time this year that the waters of the Iowa River have rushed through the streets and forced the evacuation of all 376 of Chelsea's residents.

Now, the waters have receded enough so that you can drive to the fire station and pick up cleaning supplies, but the town still has boats tied to front porch railings, carp swimming in large puddles in yards, and the smell of rotten sewage in the air. Here on a journalistic assignment, I slip my tape recorder into my pocket, sling my camera around my neck, and find my way into the Catholic school, which has been converted into a Red Cross center.

It is dinnertime, and three gray-haired women in hairnets scoop hot dogs and beans onto plastic trays in the gymnasium, Mahlon and his crew in their plain clothes sitting at one long table under the statue of Saint Jude, patron of lost and hopeless causes. Chelsea townspeople rummage through the free-clothing boxes set up in the corner of the room, plop down at tables with food, stare at the television set on one wall, tuned to the local news station showing shots of their own homes, and stare into space. Children sit docilely beside their parents, too confused to move. Parents try to attend to their children but their energy has been drained out of them like the air from a flat tire.

I interview a young couple who carried their four children high over their heads out of their flooding home, the water up to their necks.

"We can't break down," the husband and wife say in hushed voices. "We can't cry in front of our children. Instead, we fall back on our Catholic faith, our faith in God."

I interview the town mayor.

"This is an old Czech town. Catholic. I know I might catch heck for calling in the Mennonites, but they know the job and have the equipment, see?" Suddenly, the mayor looks up at me nervously, realizing I'd come to town with the disaster service and might also be a Mennonite.

"They're my neighbors. I'm an old Catholic."

"Oh." The mayor relaxes back into his chair.

I interview one of the disaster service volunteers, a woman in her thirties.

"Are you getting a sense of the town?" she asks. "Catholic." Her voice and eyes take on a hint of tension that she quickly fights off. "You might want to talk to the priest. He knows everyone and everything that goes on here."

I thank her and head down the long school corridor to find the pastor. The cornfields, which come right up to the edge of town, are decaying and stunted, having stood in water a good three months of the summer. Sofas and canning jars, piles of magazines and newspapers, photo albums and books—all the things that people keep in basements—are dumped in wet slimy clumps on their lawns in front of their houses. Clothes that have been washed three and four times but never come clean hang from the liens like dirty rags.

I am at once amazed and encouraged, amazed that this town still exists at all, having been flooded over and over for as long as its oldest residents can remember. I am amazed to think that after a hundred years, the town's religion is still its center and that that center still holds. I am also amazed that in the midst of such a disaster, religious prejudice could still crop up, could still be considered an issue. Still, I am encouraged that here today, two groups, Catholics and Protestants, whose antipathy runs deep, are working side by side.

Now I have come full circle, facing backward and forward, from one part of the state to the other, from one part of the country to another, one continent to another. I am facing backward and forward, understanding how my small experience with prejudice in my small state opened up my consciousness toward a larger world. I am facing backward and forward, wishing that we could retain our sense of community without built-in bias toward others. Now I am leaving Saint Joseph's School, the doors flung wide. I am thinking of my place at Fairview School, an outsider surrounded by a "peculiar people," people who are true outsiders to the rest of the world, people who have taken me in. Now I am wading through water toward a church, a cross on top that I see bursting into flames.

Remember Silent Stories

In this poem, Kim Uyede-Kai, whose essay about her own experience as a Japanese-Canadian opened our study, reflects on the immigrant experience of her grandmother.

Lamentations 1:1–2, 6–12
"Jerusalem remembers, in the days of her affliction and wandering, all the precious things that were hers in days of old."

My mother's mother,
my grandmother,
crippled by a stroke
when her eldest daughter
was fifteen
crippling her youth,
silencing the stories.

Stories
of a Japanese woman
married to a man she did not know
a man born in Canada
a man whose culture was her own
yet not.

Stories
of a hard life in an unknown land
a Japanese woman
isolated by language
from English neighbours
isolated by sea
from Japanese family.

Not silent then
(did she laugh?)
raising four children
her voice living on

through them
"thread for your needle
no longer than to your elbow"
"eat every grain of rice
or you will go blind."

But no stories of war
called dirty jap
enemy alien
losing the things that were home
silent pain
silent suffering.

Bedridden
silent presence
silent stories
light the Buddhist incense
at the cemetery
at the home altar.

Voiceless stories
silently scenting
the childhood of
her granddaughter
me.

Part Three
THE FUTURE:
A MULTICULTURAL NORTH AMERICA

What does the future hold? Each day is filled with new speculation, new demographic studies, new takes on the suddenly chic term "multiculturalism." We begin this section with sociologist James A. Banks' examination of the current debate within educational circles between the "multiculturalists" versus defenders of the so-called Western canon. We follow this with a display of charts from the 1990 Census setting forth the demographic distribution of ethnic groups in the United States, with the disturbing suggestion of regional balkanization. As a companion piece, we present in the brief account of one European American woman just one manifestation of such population redistribution.

On to two other essays that point us toward the future. The first is by Cornel West, African American scholar and one of the most challenging, forceful, and respected voices in the current multicultural debate. The other is by George Tinker, whom we met in the previous section of our study. We conclude with a piece by Richard Rodriguez in which he points to the multicultural future of North America, already, in his view, a fascinating and energizing reality in contemporary California.

James A. Banks

In this thoughtful and thought-provoking article, James A. Banks analyzes the current debate between those advocating changes in curriculum to reflect America's increasingly multicultural reality, and those who remain staunch adherents of the so-called Western canon. Dr. Banks is one of the world's leading scholars and researchers in the field of multicultural education. He is Professor of Education and Director of the Center for Multicultural Education at the University of Washington, Seattle.

Education within a pluralistic society should affirm and help students understand their home and community cultures. However, it should also help free them from their cultural boundaries. To create and maintain a civic community that works for the common good, education in a democratic society should help students acquire the knowledge, attitudes, and skills they will need to participate in civic action to make society more equitable and just.

Multicultural education is an education for freedom (Parekh 1986) that is essential in today's ethnically polarized and troubled world. It has evoked a divisive national debate in part because of the divergent views that citizens hold about what constitutes an American identity and about the roots and nature of American civilization. The debate in turn has sparked a power struggle over who should participate in formulating the canon used to shape the curriculum in the nation's schools, colleges, and universities.

The Debate Over the Canon

A chorus of strident voices has launched an orchestrated and widely publicized attack on the movement to infuse content about ethnic groups and women into the school and university curriculum. Much of the current debate over multicultural education has taken place in mass media publications such as *Time* (Gray 1991), *The Wall Street Journal* (Sirkin 1990), and *The New Republic* (Howe 1991), rather than in scholarly journals and forums. The Western traditionalists (writers who defend the canon now within the schools and universities) and the multiculturalists rarely engage in reflective dialogue. Rather, scholars on each side of the debate marshal data to support their briefs and ignore facts, interpretations, and perspectives that are inconsistent with their positions and visions of the present and future.

In his . . . book, *Illiberal Education*, D'Souza (1991) defends the existing curriculum and structures in higher education while presenting an alarming picture of where multiculturalism is taking the nation. When multiculturalists respond to such criticism, they often fail to describe the important ways in which the multicultural vision is consistent with the democratic ideals of the West and with the heritage of Western civilization. The multicultural literature pays too little attention to the fact that the multicultural education movement emerged out of Western democratic ideals. One of its major aims is to close the gap between the Western democratic ideals of equality and justice and societal practices that contradict those ideals, such as discrimination based on race, gender, and social class.

Because so much of the debate over the canon has taken place in the popular media, which encourages simplistic, sound-byte explanations, the issues related to the curriculum canon have been overdrawn and oversimplified by advocates on both sides. The result is that the debate often generates more heat than light. Various interest groups have been polarized rather than encouraged to exchange ideas that might help us find creative solutions to the problems related to race, ethnicity, gender, and schooling.

As the ethnic texture of the nation deepens, problems related to diversity will intensify rather than diminish. Consequently, we need leaders and educators of good will, from all political and ideological persuasions, to participate in genuine discussions, dialogue, and debates that will help us formulate visionary and workable solutions and enable us to deal creatively with the challenges posed by the increasing diversity in the United States and the world. We must learn how to transform the problems related to racial and ethnic diversity into opportunities and strengths.

Sharing Power

Western traditionalists and multiculturalists must realize that they are entering into debate from different power positions. Western traditionalists hold the balance of power, financial resources and the top positions in the mass media, in schools, colleges and universities, government, and in the publishing industry. Genuine discussion between the traditionalists and the multiculturalists can take place only when power is placed on the table, negotiated, and shared.

Despite all of the rhetoric about the extent to which Chaucer, Shakespeare, Milton, and other Western writers are threatened by the onslaught of women and writers of color into the curriculum, the reality is that the curriculum in the nation's schools and universities is largely Western in its concepts, paradigms, and content. Concepts such as the Middle Ages and the Renaissance are still used to organize most units in history, literature, and the arts. When content about African and Asian cultures is incorporated into the curriculum, it is usually viewed within the context of European concepts and paradigms. For example, Asian, African, and American histories are often studied under the topic, "The Age of Discovery," which means the time when Europeans first arrived in these continents.

Facing Realities

If they are to achieve a productive dialogue rather than a polarizing debate, both Western traditionalists and the multiculturalists must face some facts. The growing number of people of color in our society and schools constitutes a demographic imperative educators must hear and respond to. The 1990 Census indicated that one of every four Americans is a person of color. By the turn of the century, one of every three will be of color (The Commission 1988). Nearly half of the nation's students will be of color by 2020 (Pallas et al. 1989). Although the school and university curriculums remain Western-oriented, this growing number of people of color will increasingly demand to share power in curriculum decision making and in shaping a curriculum canon that reflects their experiences, histories, struggles, and victories.

People of color, women, and other marginalized groups are demanding that their voices, visions, and perspectives be included in the curriculum. They ask that the debt Western civilization owes to Africa, Asia, and indigenous America be acknowledged (Allen 1986, Bernal 1987). The advocates of the Afrocentric curriculum, in sometimes passionate language that reflects a dream long deferred, are merely asking that the cultures of Africa and African-American people be legitimized in the curriculum and that the African contributions to European civilization be acknowledged. People of color and women are also demanding that the facts about their victimization be told, for truth's sake, but also because they need to better understand their conditions so that they and others can work to reform society.

However, these groups must acknowledge that they do not want to eliminate Aristotle and Shakespeare, or Western civilization, from the school curriculum. To reject the West would be to reject important aspects of their own cultural heritages, experiences, and identities. The most important scholarly and literary works written by African-Americans, such as works by W.E.B. DuBois, Carter G. Woodson, and Zora Neale Hurston, are expressions of Western cultural experiences. African-American culture resulted from a blending of African cultural characteristics with those of African peoples in the United States.

Reinterpreting Western Civilization

Rather than excluding Western civilization from the curriculum, multiculturalists want a more truthful, complex, and diverse version of the West taught in the schools. They want the curriculum to describe the ways in which African, Asian, and indigenous American cultures have influenced and interacted with Western civilization. They also want schools to discuss not only the diversity and democratic ideals of Western civilization, but also its failures, tensions, dilemmas, and the struggles by various groups in Western societies to realize their dreams against great odds.

We need to deconstruct the myth that the West is homogeneous, that it owes few debts to other world civilizations, and that only privileged and upper-status European and European-American males have been its key actors. Weatherford (1988) describes the debt the West owes to the first Americans. Bernal (1987), Drake (1987), Sertima (1984), and Clarke (1990) marshal considerable amounts of historical and cultural data that describe the ways in which African and Afroasiatic cultures influenced the development of Western civilization. Bernal, for example, presents linguistic and archaeological evidence to substantiate his claim that important parts of Greek civilization (technologies, language, deities, and architecture) originated in ancient Africa.

We should teach students that knowledge is a social construction, that it reflects the perspectives, experiences, and the values of the people and cultures that construct it, and that it is dynamic, changing, and debated among knowledge creators and users (Banks 1991). Rather than keep such knowledge debates as the extent to which African civilizations contributed to Western civilization out of the classroom, teachers should make them an integral part of teaching. The classroom should become a forum in which multicultural debates concerning the construction or knowledge take place. The voices of the Western traditionalists, the multiculturalists, textbook authors, and radical writers should be heard and legitimized in the classroom.

Toward the Democratic Ideal

The fact that multiculturalists want to reformulate and transform the Western canon, not to purge the curriculum of the West, is absent from most of the writings of the Western traditionalists. It doesn't support their argument that Shakespeare, Milton, and Aristotle are endangered. By the same token, the multiculturalists have written little about the intersections of multicultural content and a Western-centric canon, perhaps because they have focused on ways in which the established Western canon should be reconstructed and transformed.

Multicultural education itself is a product of the West. It grew out of a struggle guided by Western ideals for human dignity, equality, and freedom (Parker 1991). Multicultural education is a child of the civil rights movement led by African Americans that was designed to eliminate discrimination in housing, public accommodation, and other areas. The leaders of the civil rights movement, such as Fannie Lou Hamer, Rosa Parks, and Daisy Bates, internalized the American democratic ideal stated in such important United States documents as the Declaration of Independence, the Constitution, and the Bill of Rights. The civil rights leaders of the 1960s and 1970s used the Western ideals of freedom and democracy to justify and legitimize their push for structural inclusion and the end of institutionilized discrimination and racism.

The civil rights movement of the 1960s echoed throughout the United States and the world. Other groups, such as Native Americans and Hispanics, women, and people with disabilities, initiated their own freedom movements. These cultural revitalization movements made demands on a number of institutions. The nation's schools and universities became primary targets for reform, in part because they were important symbols of the structural exclusion that victimized groups experienced, and in part because they were easily accessible.

It would be a serious mistake to interpret these cultural revitalization movements and the educational reforms they gave birth to as a repudiation of the West and Western civilization. The major goals of these movements are full inclusion of the victimized groups into Western institutions and a reform of these institutions so that their practices are more consistent with their democratic ideals. Multicultural education not only arose out of Western traditions and ideals, its major goal is to create a nation-state that actualizes the democratic ideals for all that the Founding Fathers intended for an elite few. Rather than being divisive as some critics contend, multicultural education is designed to reduce race, class, and gender divisions in the United States and the world.

Given the tremendous social class and racial cleavages in United States society, it is inaccurate to claim that the study of ethnic diversity will threaten national cohesion. The real threats to national unity—which in an economic, sociological, and psychological sense we have not fully attained but are working toward—are the deepening racial and social-class schisms within United States society. As Wilson (1987) points out in *The Truly Disadvantaged*, the gap between the rich and the poor has grown tremendously in recent years. The social-class schism has occurred not

References

Allen, P. G. (1986). *The Sacred Hoop, Recovering the Feminine in American Indian Traditions.* Beacon Press.

Banks, J. A. (1991). *Teaching Strategies for Ethnic Studies,* 5th ed. Boston: Allyn and Bacon.

Bernal, M. (1987). *The Afroasiatic Roots of Classical Civilization,* Vol. 1: *The Fabrication of Ancient Greece 1785-1985.* London: Free Association Books.

Clarke, J. H. (1990). "African People on My Mind." In *Infusion of African and African American Content in the School Curriculum: Proceedings of the First National Conference,* edited by A.G. Hilliard III, L. Payton-Stewart, and L.O. Williams. Morristown, N.J.: Aaron Press.

The Commission on Minority Participation in Education and American Life. (May 1988). *One-Third of a Nation.* Washington, D.C.: The American Council on Education.

D'Souza, D. (1991). *Illiberal Education: The Politics of Race and Sex on Campus.* New York: The Free Press.

Drake, St. C. (1987). *Black Folk Here and There.* Vol. 1. Los Angeles: Center for Afro-American Studies, University of California.

Gray, P. (July 8, 1991). "Whose America?" *Time* 138: 13-17.

Greene, M. (1988). *The Dialectic of Freedom.* New York: Teachers College Press.

BIGGEST BLACK METROS

(metropolitan statistical areas ranked by size of black population in 1990)

rank / metro area	1990 black population	rank / metro area	1990 black population
1 New York, NY	2,250,026	15 Norfolk-Virginia Beach-Newport News, VA	398,093
2 Chicago, IL	1,332,919	16 Miami-Hialeah, FL	397,993
3 Washington, DC-MD VA	1,041,934	17 Cleveland, OH	355,619
4 Los Angeles-Long Beach, CA	992,974	18 Oakland, CA	303,826
5 Detroit, MI	943,479	19 Richmond-Petersburg, VA	252,340
6 Philadelphia, PA-NJ	929,907	20 Birmingham AL	245,726
7 Atlanta, GA	736,153	21 Boston-Lawrence-Salem-Lowell-Brockton, MA	233,819
8 Baltimore, MD	616,065	22 Charlotte-Gastonia-Rock Hill, NC-SC	231,654
9 Houston, TX	611,243	23 Kansas City, MO-KS	200,508
10 New Orleans, LA	430,470	24 Milwaukee, WI	197,183
11 St. Louis, MO-IL	423,185	25 Nassau-Suffolk, NY	193,967
12 Newark, NJ	422,802		
13 Dallas, TX	410,766		
14 Memphis, TN-AR-MS	399,011		

BIGGEST HISPANIC METROS

(metropolitan statistical areas ranked by Hispanic population in 1990)

rank / metro area	1990 Hispanic population	rank / metro area	1990 Hisapanic population
1 Los Angeles-Long Beach, CA	3,351,242	14 San Jose, CA	314,564
2 New York, NY	1,889,662	15 Oakland, CA	273,087
3 Miami-Hialeah, FL	953,407	16 Fresno, CA	236,634
4 Chicago, IL	734,827	17 San Francisco, CA	233,274
5 Houston, TX	707,536	18 Washington, DC-MD-VA	224.786
6 Riverside-San Bernardino, CA	686,096	19 Brownsville-Harlingen, TX	212,995
7 San Antonio, TX	620,290	20 Denver, CO	211,005
8 Anaheim-Santa Ana, CA	564,828	21 Newark, NJ	188,299
9 San Diego, CA	510,781	22 Boston-Lawrence-Salem-Lowell-Brockton, MA	186,652
10 El Paso, TX	411,619	23 Jersey City, NJ	183,465
11 Dallas, TX	368,884	24 Corpus Christi, TX	181,860
12 Phoenix, AZ	345,498	25 Albuquerque, NM	178,310
13 McAllen-Edinburg-Mission, TX	326,972		

BIGGEST ASIAN METROS (U.S.A.)

(metropolitan statistical areas ranked by Asian-American population in 1990)

rank / metro area	1990 Asian population	rank / metro area	1990 Asian population
1 Los Angeles-Long Beach, CA	954,485	16 Riverside-San Bernardino, CA	100,792
2 New York, NY	556,399	17 Dallas, TX	67,195
3 Honolulu, HI	526,459	18 Bergen-Passaic, NJ	66,743
4 San Francisco, CA	329,599	19 Minneapolis-St. Paul, MN-WI	65,204
5 Oakland, CA	269,566	20 Nassau-Suffolk, NY	62,399
6 San Jose, CA	261,466	21 Stockton, CA	59,690
7 Anaheim-Santa Ana, CA	249,192	22 Detroit, MI	57,730
8 Chicago, IL	229,492	23 Fresno, CA	57,239
9 Washington, DC-MD-VA	202,437	24 Middlesex-Somerset-Hunterdon, NJ	56,804
10 San Diego, CA	198,311	25 Newark, NJ	52,898
11 Seattle, WA	135,251	26 Atlanta, GA	51,486
12 Houston, TX	126,601	27 Vallejo-Fairfield-Napa, CA	47,044
13 Boston-Lawrence-Salem-Lowell-Brockton, MA	116,597	28 Portland, OR	46,360
14 Sacramento, CA	114,520	29 Baltimore, MD	42,634
15 Philadelphia, PA-NJ	104,595	30 Denver, CO	37,134

THE MOST DIVERSE COUNTIES

(rank of counties where proportions of non-Hispanic whites, non-Hispanic blacks, Hispanics, and non-Hispanics other races are nearest to being equal, 1990)

rank / county	state	rank / county	state
1 Queens County	New York	26 Kings County	California
2 San Francisco County	California	27 Dallas County	Texas
3 Los Angeles County	California	28 Suffolk County	Massachusetts
4 Kings County	New York	29 Hendry County	Florida
5 Alameda County	California	30 Matagorda County	Texas
6 New York County	New York	31 Graham County	Arizona
7 Bronx County	New York	32 Denver County	Colorado
8 Hudson County	New Jersey	33 San Juan County	New Mexico
9 Fort Bend County	Texas	34 San Bernardino County	California
10 Cibola County	New Mexico	35 Socorro County	New Mexico
11 Harris County	Texas	36 Aleutians West Census Area	Alaska
12 Robeson County	North Carolina	37 Passaic County	New Jersey
13 Solano County	California	38 Pinal County	Arizona
14 Essex County	New Jersey	39 Alexandria (city)	Virginia
15 Dade County	Florida	40 Waller County	Texas
16 Sandoval County	New Mexico	41 Caldwell County	Texas
17 Monterey County	California	42 San Diego County	California
18 Fresno County	California	43 Liberty County	Georgia
19 San Joaquin County	California	44 Prince George's County	Maryland
20 Santa Clara County	California	45 Wharton County	Texas
21 San Mateo County	California	46 Philadelphia County	Pennsylvania
22 Cook County	Illinois	47 Bell County	Texas
23 Merced County	California	48 Otero County	New Mexico
24 Hoke County	North Carolina	49 Union County	New Jersey
25 Chattahooche County	Georgia		

Canadian Population by Mother Tongue[1]
(thousands of persons and percent of total population)

	1941	%	1951	%	1961	%	1971	%	1981	%	1991	%
English	6,448	56.0	8,281	59.1	10,661	58.5	12,974	60.2	14.918	61.3	16 170	60.0
French	3,355	29.2	4,069	29.0	5,123	28.1	5,794	26.9	6,249	25.7	6 503	24.1
Italian	80	0.7	92	0.7	340	1.9	538	2.5	529	2.2	511	1.9
German	322	2.8	329	2.3	564	3.1	561	2.6	523	2.2	466	1.7
Chinese	34	0.3	28	0.2	49	0.3	95	0.4	224	0.9	499	1.8
Ukranian	313	2.7	352	2.5	361	2.0	310	1.4	292	1.2	187	.7
Portuguese	n.a.	n.a.	n.a.	n.a.	18	0.1	87	0.4	166	0.7	212	.8
Dutch	53	0.5	88	0.6	170	0.9	145	0.7	157	0.6	139	.5
Polish	129	1.1	129	0.9	162	0.9	135	0.6	128	0.5	190	.7
Greek	9	0.1	8	0.1	40	0.2	104	0.5	123	0.5	126	.5
Spanish	1	--	2	--	7	--	24	0.1	70	0.3	177	.7
Indo-Iranian	--	--	2	--	5	--	33	0.2	117	0.5	301	1.1
Aboriginal	131	1.1	166	1.2	167	0.9	180	0.9	146	0.6	173	.6
Hungarian	46	0.4	42	0.3	86	0.5	87	0.4	84	0.3	80	.3
Vietnamese	n.a.	n.a.	n.a.	n.a.	n.a.	n.a.	n.a.	n.a.	30	0.1	79	.3
Arabic	8	0.1	5	--	13	0.1	29	0.1	50	0.2	108	.4
Finnish	37	0.3	32	0.2	45	0.2	37	0.2	33	0.1	28	.1
Russian	52	0.5	39	0.3	43	0.2	32	0.1	31	0.1	35	.1
Yiddish	130	1.1	104	0.7	82	0.4	50	0.2	33	0.1	25	.09
Czech[2]	38	0.3	46	0.3	51	0.3	45	0.2	43	0.2	27	.09
Danish	19	0.2	16	0.1	35	0.2	27	0.1	26	0.1	22	.08
Japanese	22	0.2	18	0.1	18	0.1	17	0.1	20	0.1	30	.1
Armenian	n.a.	n.a.	n.a.	n.a.	n.a.	n.a.	n.a.	n.a.	17	0.1	26	.1
Norwegian	60	0.5	44	0.3	40	0.2	27	0.1	19	0.1	13	.05
Swedish	50	0.4	36	0.3	33	0.2	22	0.1	17	0.1	12	.04

Source: *Census of Canada*
[1]The language first spoken in childhood and still understood.
[2]Includes Slovak.
(n.a.) not available. (--) too small to be lncluded.

NATIVE POPULATION OF CANADA

	1986				1991			
	Total Native Population[21]	Native Indian	Métis	Inuit	Total Population with Aboriginal Origins[12]	Native Indian	Métis	Inuit
Canada	711 725	548 945	151 605	36 460	1 002 675	783 980	212 650	49 255
Newfoundland	9 555	4 695	1 435	4 120	13 110	5 845	1 605	6 460
Prince Edward Island	1 290	1 115	160	30	1 880	1 665	185	75
Nova Scotia	14 225	13 060	1 110	315	21 885	19 950	1 590	770
New Brunswick	9 375	8 700	750	185	12 815	11 835	975	450
Quebec	80 945	68 585	11 435	7 360	137 615	112 590	19 480	8 480
Ontario	167 375	150 715	18 265	2 955	243 550	220 135	26 905	5 250
Manitoba	85 235	55 960	33 285	700	116 200	76 370	45 575	900
Saskatchewan	77 650	55 215	25 695	190	96 580	69 385	32 840	540
Alberta	103 925	68 965	40 125	1 125	148 220	99 650	56 310	2 825
British Columbia	126 625	112 790	15 295	1 035	169 035	149 570	22 295	1 990
Yukon	4 995	4 775	220	65	6 390	5 870	565	170
Northwest Territories	30 530	9 380	3 825	18 360	35 390	11 100	4 310	21 355

Source: *Census of Canada*
1. The 1991 census question on ethnic or cultural origins gathered information on the number of people who reported North American Indian, Métis, or Inuit origin as either a single response or in combination with other origins.

2. 1986 census excluded approximately 45 000 individuals living on incompletely enumerated native reserves and settlements; in 1991 census, 78 reserves were incompletely enumerated, representing approximately 37 000 individuals.

Canadian Population by Country of Birth

	1911	1931	1951	1971	1991
Total Population	7 206 643	10 376 786	14 009 429	21 588 310	27 294 855
Total Foreign Born	1 586 961	2 307 525	2 059 911	3 295 530	4 335 185
Africa - Other	--	--	--	--	42 245
Argentina	--	--	--	--	11 110
Asia - Other	3 577	6 310	6 740	52 795	85 705
Australia	2 655	3 565	4 161	14 335	13 955
Austria	121 430	37 391	37 598	40 450	26 680
Barbados	--	--	--	--	14 820
Belgium	7 975	17 033	17 251	25 770	22 480
Brazil	--	--	--	--	7 325
Carribean - Other	--	--	--	--	25 990
Central America - Other--	--	--	--	21 120	
Chile	--	- -	--	--	22 870
China	27 083	42 037	24 166	57 150	157 405
Czechoslovakia	--	22 835	29 546	43 100	42 615
Denmark	4 937	17 217	15 679	28 045	21 555
Ecuador	--	--	--	--	8 015
Egypt					28 015
El Salvador	--	--	--	--	28 295
Ethiopia	--	--	--	--	11 060
Europe - Other	12 394	10 657	10 858	87 255	9 215
Fiji					16 000
Finland	10 987	30 354	22 035	24 930	16 830
France	17 619	16 756	15 650	51 655	55 160
Germany	39 577	39 163	42 693	211 060	180 525
Greece	2 640	5 579	8 594	78 780	83 675
Guyana	--	--	--	--	66 055
Haiti	--	--	--	--	39 880
Hong Kong	--	--	--	--	152 455
Hungary	--	28 523	32 929	68 495	57 010
India	4 491	4 672	3 934	43 645	173 670
Iran	--	--	--	--	30 715
Ireland	--	--	24 110	38 490	28 405
Israel	--	--	--	--	16 770
Italy	34 739	42 578	57 789	385 755	351 620
Jamaica	--	--	--	--	102 440
Japan	8 425	12 261	6 239	9 485	12 280
Kenya	--	--	--	--	16 585
Korea	--	--	--	--	33 170
Laos	--	--	--	--	14 445
Lebanon	--	--	--	--	54 605
Malaysia	--	--	--	--	16 100
Malta	--	--	--	—	10 185
Mexico	--	--	--	--	19 400
Morocco	--	--	--	--	16 795
Netherlands	3 808	10 736	41 457	133 525	129 615
New Zealand	903	---	--	--	7 480
North America - Other	--	--	--	--	455
Norway	20 968	32 679	22 969	16 350	8 260
Oceania - Other	--	--	--	--	545
Pakistan	--	--	--	--	25 180
Philippines	--	--	--	--	123 295

Howe, I. (February 18, 1991). "The Value of the Canon." *The New Republic*: 40-44.

Pallas, A. M., G. Natriello, E.L. McDill. (June-July 1989). "The Changing Nature of the Disadvantaged Population: Current Dimensions and Future Trends." *Educational Researcher* 18, 2:2.

Parekh, B. (1986). "The Concept of Multi-Cultural Education." In *Multicultural Education: The Interminable Debate*, edited by S. Modgil, G. K. Verma, K. Mallick, and C. Modgil. Philadelphia: The Falmer Press, pp. 19-31.

Parker, W. P. (1991). "Multicultural Education in Democratic Societies." Paper presented at the annual meeting of the American Educational Research Association, Chicago.

Sirkin, G. (January 18, 1990). "The Multiculturalists Strike Again." *The Wall Street Journal*, p. A14.

Sertima, I.V., ed. (1984). (Ed). *Black Women in Antiquity*. New Brunswick, N.J.: Transaction Books.

Weatherford, J. (1988*). Indian Givers: How the Indians of the Americas Transformed the World*. New York: Fawcett Columbine.

Wilson, W. J. (1987). *The Truly Disadvantaged: The Inner City, the Underclass, and Public Policy*. Chicago: the University of Chicago Press.

only across racial and ethnic groups, but within these groups. Hence, the rush to the suburbs has not just been a white flight, but has been a flight by the middle class of many hues. As a consequence, low-income African Americans and Hispanics have been left in inner-city communities without the middle-class members of their groups to provide needed leadership and role models. They are more excluded than ever from mainstream American society.

Educating for Freedom

Each of us becomes culturally encapsulated during our socialization in childhood. We accept the assumptions of our own community culture, internalize its values, views of the universe, misconceptions, and stereotypes. Although this is as true for the child socialized within a mainstream culture as it is for the minority child, minority children are usually forced to examine, confront, and question their cultural assumptions when they enter school.

Students who are born and socialized within the mainstream culture of a society rarely have an opportunity to identify, question, and challenge their cultural assumptions, beliefs, values, and perspectives because the school culture usually reinforces those that they learn at home and in their communities. Consequently, mainstream Americans have few opportunities to become free of cultural assumptions and perspectives that are monocultural, that devalue African and Asian cultures, and that stereotype people of color and people who are poor, or who are victimized in other ways. These mainstream Americans often have an inability to function effectively within other American cultures, and lack the ability and motivation to experience and benefit from cross-cultural participation and relationships.

To fully participate in our democratic society, these students and all students need the skills a multicultural education can give them to understand others and to thrive in a rapidly changing, diverse world. Thus, the debate between the Western traditionalists and the multiculturalists fits well within the tradition of a pluralistic democratic society. Its final result will most likely be not exactly what either side wants, but a synthesized and compromised perspective that will provide a new vision for the nation as we enter the 21st century.

William H. Frey and Jonathan Tilove

By telling the story of one European American woman, this brief article suggests how the kind of population distribution laid out in the demographic charts developed from the 1990 Census is manifesting itself. The piece, written by William H. Frey and Jonathan Tilove, appeared in The New York Times Magazine, *August 20, 1995. William H. Frey is a demographer who teaches sociology at the University of Michigan. Jonathan Tilove writes about race relations for Newhouse News Service.*

Three years ago, Marilyn Yarosko moved to Las Vegas; she was feeling out of place in her native Southern California. The Asian population in her hometown of Torrance, just south of Los Angeles, had doubled to 22 percent in the 1980's. The pastor and most of the parishioners at her Roman Catholic church were now Vietnamese. Most of her fellow nurses at Charter Suburban Hospital, she says, were Filipino, super-hardworking and, she thinks, a bit cliquish. Yarosko, whose parents were Canadian and paternal grandparents were from the Ukraine, is not a xenophobe. She is not bitter or looking for someone to blame. "We took it from the Indians: who are we to complain?" she says. But, she acknowledges, "I began to feel like an outsider."

"For every white person who leaves," she says of Los Angeles, "a foreigner takes their place."

Her remark is not merely an anecdotal insight. A new analysis of the 1990 United States Census discloses that some of America's largest metropolitan areas are experiencing something statistically very close to Yarosko's observation: For every immigrant who arrives, a white person leaves. Look collectively at the New York, Chicago, Los Angeles, Houston and Boston metropolitan areas—5 of the top 11 immigration destinations. In the last half of the 80's, for every 10 immigrants who arrived, 9 residents left for points elsewhere. And most of those leaving were non-Hispanic whites. Of the top immigrant destinations, only metropolitan San Diego was attracting more whites from the rest of the nation than it was losing. The places that whites were bound for were metro areas like Tampa-St. Petersburg, Seattle, Phoenix, Atlanta and Las Vegas, all of which attract relatively few immigrants.

The trend constitutes a new, larger form of white flight. Unlike in the old version, whites this time are not just fleeing the cities for the suburbs. They are leaving entire metropolitan areas and states—whole regions— for whiter destinations. And new census estimates indicate that this pattern of flight from big immigration destinations has become even more pronounced in the 90's.

This combination of concentrated minority immigration and distinctly white dispersal is reshaping America more and more into two nations. One is the rapidly changing, intensely diverse America represented by the coastal ports of entry from San Francisco to Houston in the West, and Boston to Washington plus Miami in the East, along with the premier Middle Western destination of Chicago. The second is the rest of the country, experiencing this new diversity in modest numbers or not at all. In other words, the old image of immigrant assimilation is being supplanted by a new one—Balkanization.

The force behind all this change is a decade of greater immigration, and greater minority immigration, than any in American history. According to the Urban Institute, a research organization in Washington, some 10 million legal and illegal immigrants entered the country in the 80's, exceeding the previous high of 9 million recorded in the first decade of the century. The relative rate of immigration is obviously much lower now; the population is also now three times as large.

Nevertheless, today's geographic concentration of immigrants is much higher. More than three-quarters of immigrants in the 1980's settled in just six states, and more than half of those immigrants were in just eight metropolitan areas.

Moreover, unlike past eras of immigration, this new wave is more than 80 percent Latin American and Asian. Most immigrants arrive to discover that they are officially classified as members of a racial group—usually Hispanic or Asian. Legally and culturally, they are all defined as minorities—just as blacks have been, even though most blacks originally came to America as slaves. In California, this pattern has altered the dynamics of affirmative action in ways that go unrecognized in the currently raging debate on the subject. Because of immigration, in the 30-odd years since the dawn of affirmative action, blacks have gone from more than two-thirds to less than half of America's minority population.

Nationally, black workers, and especially the black middle class, are disproportionately concentrated in government jobs. But with substantial numbers of new immigrants arriving, blacks in these port-of-entry cities find themselves increasingly overrepresented in government jobs vis-à-vis their shrinking percentage of the minority population. The result: The new minorities' affirmative-action claims for fairness can't help but come at the expense of blacks.

Ultimately, this interplay of immigration and affirmative action encourages Americans to identify themselves by race and ancestry, and when necessary, move to where that identity serves them best. It's happening. According to the 1990 census, blacks, like whites, are also leaving most of the high-immigration metropolitan areas, if not in the same numbers as whites, and their No. 1 destination is Atlanta. By contrast, the No. 1 destination for Hispanic-Americans is Miami, and the No. 1 destination for Asian-Americans is Los Angeles.

Meanwhile, the whites leaving high-immigration metropolitan areas are those most likely to be competing with immigrants for jobs, space and cultural primacy. Classically, those most likely to move are the most affluent and best educated; now it is the less affluent, less well-educated whites. They are not the ones who can afford to hire immigrants to mind their kids, trim their hedges and make their hotel beds. They are the whites whose neighborhoods and public school classrooms are visibly changing, and the ones most likely to be economically displaced by immigrants who pour in no matter how lousy the local economy may be. What they leave behind is a society more racially stratified, with affluent whites on top in their gated communities and private schools, and minorities at the bottom, competing with one another for jobs, turf and power.

Those who leave are not just switching neighborhoods. Consider California. It will be less than half white within a decade because of a massive influx of minority immigrants and a disproportionately white exodus, mostly to neighboring states, which are among the whitest in the nation. In Las Vegas, most of Marilyn Yarosko's neighbors and co-workers are white. Gone is any sense of identity or community Yarosko had with those she left behind. For now, when someone like Yarosko flees Los Angeles for Las Vegas, she is not just leaving one state for another, she is leaving one America for another.

Cornel West

Cornel West speaks passionately, in this introduction to his book **Race Matters,** *about the urgent need for American society to launch a serious, critical, and candid engagement with the complex issue of race. Dr. West is Professor of Afro-American Studies and the Phi-*

*losophy of Religion at Harvard University. He is an influential au-
thor and widely respected voice in the current multicultural debate.*

What happened in Los Angeles in April of 1992 was neither a race riot
nor a class rebellion. Rather, this monumental upheaval was a multiracial, trans-class, and largely male display of justified social rage. For all
its ugly, xenophobic resentment, its air of adolescent carnival, and its
downright barbaric behavior, it signified the sense of powerlessness in
American society. Glib attempts to reduce its meaning to the pathologies
of the black underclass, the criminal actions of hoodlums, or the political
revolt of the oppressed urban masses miss the mark. Of those arrested,
only 36 percent were black, more than a third had full-time jobs, and
most claimed to shun political affiliation. What we witnessed in Los Angeles was the consequence of a lethal linkage of economic decline, cultural decay, and political lethargy in American life. Race was the visible
catalyst, not the underlying cause.

The meaning of the earthshaking events in Los Angeles is difficult to
grasp because most of us remain trapped in the narrow framework of the
dominant liberal and conservative views of race in America, which with
its worn-out vocabulary leaves us intellectually debilitated, morally
disempowered, and personally depressed. The astonishing disappearance
of the event from public dialogue is testimony to just how painful and
distressing a serious engagement with race is. Our truncated public discussions of race suppress the best of who and what we are as a people
because they fail to confront the complexity of the issue in a candid and
critical manner. The predictable pitting of liberals against conservatives,
Great Society Democrats against self-help Republicans, reinforces intellectual parochialism and political paralysis.

The liberal notion that more government programs can solve racial
problems is simplistic—precisely because it focuses *solely* on the economic
dimension. And the conservative idea that what is needed is a change in
the moral behavior of poor black urban dwellers (especially poor black
men, who, they say, should stay married, support their children, and stop
committing so much crime) highlights immoral actions while ignoring
public responsibility for the immoral circumstances that haunt our fellow
citizens.

The common denominator of these views of race is that each still sees
black people as a "problem people," in the words of Dorothy I. Height,
president of the National Council of Negro Women, rather than as fellow
American citizens with problems. Her words echo the poignant "unasked
question" of W. E. B. Du Bois, who, in *The Souls of Black Folk* (1903), wrote:

> They approach me in a half-hesitant sort of way, eye me curi-
> ously or compassionately, and then instead of saying directly,
> How does it feel to be a problem? they say, I know an excellent
> colored man in my town. . . . Do not these Southern outrages
> make your blood boil? At these I smile, or am interested, or
> reduce the boiling to a simmer, as the occasion may require. To
> the real question, How does it feel to be a problem? I answer
> seldom a word.

Nearly a century later, we confine discussions about race in America
to the "problems" black people pose for whites, rather than consider what

this way of viewing black people reveals about us as a nation.

This paralyzing framework encourages liberals to relieve their guilty consciences by supporting public funds directed at "the problems"; but at the same time, reluctant to exercise principled criticism of black people, liberals deny them the freedom to err. Similarly, conservatives blame the "problems" on black people themselves—and thereby render black social misery invisible or unworthy of public attention.

Hence, for liberals, black people are to be "included" and "integrated" into "our" society and culture, while for conservatives they are to be "well behaved" and "worthy of acceptance" by "our" way of life. Both fail to see that the presence and predicaments of black people are neither additions to nor defections from American life, but rather *constitutive elements of that life.*

To engage in a serious discussion of race in America, we must begin not with the problems of black people but with the flaws of American society—flaws rooted in historic inequalities and longstanding cultural stereotypes. How we set up the terms for discussing racial issues shapes our perception and response to these issues. As long as black people are viewed as a "them," the burden falls on blacks to do all the "cultural" and "moral" work necessary for healthy race relations. The implication is that only certain Americans can define what it means to be American—and the rest must simply "fit in."

The emergence of strong black-nationalist sentiments among blacks, especially among young people, is a revolt against this sense of having to "fit in." The variety of black-nationalist ideologies, from the moderate views of Supreme Court Justice Clarence Thomas in his youth to those of Louis Farrakhan today, rest upon a fundamental truth: white America has been historically weak-willed in ensuring racial justice and has continued to resist fully accepting the humanity of blacks. As long as double standards and differential treatment abound—as long as the rap performer Ice-T is harshly condemned while former Los Angeles Police Chief Daryl F. Gates's antiblack comments are received in polite silence, as long as Dr. Leonard Jeffries's anti-Semitic statements are met with vitriolic outrage while presidential candidate Patrick J. Buchanan's anti-Semitism receives a genteel response—black nationalisms will thrive.

Afrocentrism, a contemporary species of black nationalism, is a gallant yet misguided attempt to define an African identity in a white society perceived to be hostile. It is gallant because it puts black doings and sufferings, not white anxieties and fears, at the center of discussion. It is misguided because—out of fear of cultural hybridization and through silence on the issue of class, retrograde views on black women, gay men, and lesbians, and a reluctance to link race to the common good—it reinforces the narrow discussions about race.

To establish a new framework, we need to begin with a frank acknowledgment of the basic humanness and Americanness of each of us. And we must acknowledge that as a people—*E Pluribus Unum*—we are on a slippery slope toward economic strife, social turmoil, and cultural chaos. If we go down, we go down together. The Los Angeles upheaval forced us to see not only that we are not connected in ways we would like to be but also, in a more profound sense, that this failure to connect binds us even more tightly together. The paradox of race in America is that our common destiny is more pronounced and imperiled precisely when our divisions are deeper. The Civil War and its legacy speak loudly here. And our divisions are growing deeper. Today, 86 percent of white suburban Americans live in neighborhoods that are less than 1 percent black, meaning that the prospects for the country depend largely on how its cities fare in the hands of a suburban electorate. There is no escape from our interracial interdependence, yet enforced racial hierarchy dooms us as a nation to collective paranoia and hysteria—the unmaking of any democratic order.

The verdict in the Rodney King case, which sparked the incidents in Los Angeles, was perceived to be wrong by the vast majority of Americans. But whites have often failed to acknowledge the widespread mistreatment of black people, especially black men, by law enforcement agencies, which helped ignite the spark. The verdict was merely the occasion for deep-seated rage to come to the surface. This rage is fed by the "silent" depression ravaging the country—in which real weekly wages of all American workers since 1973 have declined nearly 20 percent, while at the same time wealth has been upwardly distributed.

The exodus of stable industrial jobs from urban centers to cheaper labor markets here and abroad, housing policies that have created "chocolate cities and vanilla suburbs" (to use the popular musical artist George Clinton's memorable phrase), white fear of black crime, and the urban influx of poor Spanish-speaking and Asian immigrants—all have helped erode the tax base of American cities just as the federal government has cut its support and programs. The result is unemployment, hunger, homelessness, and sickness for millions.

And a pervasive spiritual impoverishment grows. The collapse of meaning in life—the eclipse of hope and absence of love of self and others, the breakdown of family and neighborhood bonds—leads to the social deracination and cultural denudement of urban dwellers, especially children. We have created rootless, dangling people with little link to the supportive networks—family, friends, school—that sustain some sense of purpose in life. We have witnessed the collapse of the spiritual communities that in the past helped Americans face despair, disease, and death and that transmit through the generations dignity and decency, excellence and elegance.

The result is lives of what we might call "random nows," of fortuitous and fleeting moments preoccupied with "getting over"—with acquiring pleasure, property, and power by any means necessary. (This is not what Malcolm X meant by this famous phrase.) Post-modern culture is more and more a market culture dominated by gangster mentalities and self-destructive wantonness. This culture engulfs all of us—yet its impact on the disadvantaged is devastating, resulting in extreme violence in everyday life. Sexual violence against women and homicidal assaults by young black men on one another are only the most obvious signs of this empty quest for pleasure, property, and power.

Last, this rage is fueled by a political atmosphere in which images, not ideas, dominate, where politicians spend more time raising money than debating issues. The functions of parties have been displaced by public polls, and politicians behave less as thermostats that determine the climate of opinion than as thermometers registering the public mood. American politics has been rocked by an unleashing of greed among opportunistic public officials—who have followed the lead of their counterparts in the private sphere, where, as of 1989, 1 percent of the population owned 37 percent of the wealth and 10 percent of the population owned 86 percent of the wealth—leading to a profound cynicism and pessimism among the citizenry. . . .

What is to be done? How do we capture a new spirit and vision to meet the challenges of the post-industrial city, post-modern culture, and post-party politics?

First, we must admit that the most valuable sources for help, hope, and power consist of ourselves and our common history. As in the ages of Lincoln, Roosevelt, and King, we must look to new frameworks and languages to understand our multilayered crisis and overcome our deep malaise.

Second, we must focus our attention on the public square—the common good that undergirds our national and global destinies. The vitality of any public square ultimately depends on how much we *care* about the quality of our lives together. The neglect of our public infrastructure, for example—our water and sewage systems, bridges, tunnels, highways, subways, and streets—reflects not only our myopic economic policies, which impede productivity, but also the low priority we place on our common life.

The tragic plight of our children clearly reveals our deep disregard for public well-being. About one out of every five children in this country lives in poverty, including one out of every two black children and two out of every five Hispanic children. Most of our children—neglected by overburdened parents and bombarded by the market values of profit-hungry corporations—are ill-equipped to live lives of spiritual and cultural quality. Faced with these facts, how do we expect ever to constitute a vibrant society?

One essential step is some form of large-scale public intervention to ensure access to basic social goods—housing, food, health care, education, child care, and jobs. We must invigorate the common good with a mixture of government, business, and labor that does not follow any existing blueprint. After a period in which the private sphere has been sacralized and the public square gutted, the temptation is to make a fetish of the public square. We need to resist such dogmatic swings.

Last, the major challenge is to meet the need to generate new leadership. The paucity of courageous leaders—so apparent in the response to the events in Los Angeles—requires that we look beyond the same elites and voices that recycle the older frameworks. We need leaders—neither saints nor sparkling television personalities—who can situate themselves within a larger historical narrative of this country and our world, who can grasp the complex dynamics of our peoplehood and imagine a future grounded in the best of our past, yet who are attuned to the frightening obstacles that now perplex us. Our ideals of freedom, democracy, and equality must be invoked to invigorate all of us, especially the landless, propertyless, and luckless. Only a visionary leadership that can motivate "the better angels of our nature," as Lincoln said, and activate possibilities for a freer, more efficient, and stable America—only that leadership deserves cultivation and support.

This new leadership must be grounded in grass-roots organizing that highlights democratic accountability. Whoever *our* leaders will be as we approach the twenty-first century, their challenge will be to help Americans determine whether a genuine multiracial democracy can be created and sustained in an era of global economy and a moment of xenophobic frenzy.

Let us hope and pray that the vast intelligence, imagination, humor, and courage of Americans will not fail us. Either we learn a new language of empathy and compassion, or the fire this time will consume us all.

George E. Tinker

George E. Tinker, whose analysis of the missionary enterprise we presented in the previous section, asks important questions about future relations between Native Americans and other, primarily European American, residents of the United States. This material, like the previous selection, comes from Dr. Tinker's book Missionary Conquest: The Gospel and Native American Cultural Genocide.

American Indian peoples need their white friends today more than ever. What we need, however, are genuine friends, not self-proclaimed friends who know what is best for us. We do not need so-called friends who would invite themselves in to pillage the remaining treasures of Indian spirituality, or well-meaning liberals who would try to show us how to make the system work for Indians. Rather, we need friends who will join us in the struggle against the continuing imperialism of Western, European-American culture. Genuine friends do not invade one another, physically or spiritually. Genuine friends do not prescribe for one another. But genuine friends do stand beside one another, supporting one another in times of need and crisis.

Yes, American Indians need friends today, but we need friends who will fight political battles within their own political system, not friends who have abandoned the political struggle in favor of a retreat to some reservation nirvana where all their problems dissipate into a cloud of spiritual smoke.

A curious reversal has seemingly occurred in the attitudes of many white Americans and Europeans toward Native American peoples. One of the more significant problems faced by Indian peoples today is not the intentional and overt imposition of European culture in the guise of Christianity. Nor is it the federal legislation or policy that made many tribal ceremonies illegal or the official church and state displeasure that made nearly all ceremonies difficult to sustain.[1] Rather, our modern problem is just the opposite of the problem the tribes confronted a century ago in the presence of the missionary. Nevertheless, in a subtle way, the systemic imposition of Euroamerican culture on Indian peoples persist. Paradoxically, the modern appeal of Indian spirituality to many white people has, I believe, become a major destructive force in our Indian communities. The withering of white Christian spirituality has so disillusioned people that many have engaged in a relatively intense search for something to fill the spiritual void, from Buddhism, Sufi mysticism, or Hindu meditation to Lynn Andrews hucksterism[2] or the so-called "men's council" movement, with channeling, astrology, and witchcraft falling somewhere in between. In this time of spiritual crisis, Indian spirituality, which just a short while ago was the anathema of heathenism, has now become an appealing alternative to many of the seekers.

The main difficulty is that Indian spiritual traditions are still rooted in cultural contexts that are quite foreign to white Euroamericans, yet Euroamerican cultural structures are the only devices Euroamericans have for any deep structure understanding of native spiritual traditions. Hence, those native traditions can only be understood by analogy with white experience. To use a paradigm devised by linguist Noam Chomsky over three decades ago, Indian and white people may see an identical surface structure, yet understand that surface structure in radically different ways because they are rooted in culturally disparate deep structures.[3] To make matters even more confusing, the two may go along for a long time without recognizing the deep structure differences in understanding. A simple example may suffice to demonstrate the potential for complex cultural differentiation. The sentence, "The girl hit the boy with the bat," is a single surface structure, yet it equally represents two quite different deep structure perceptions of reality. Without further investigation, one is left wondering whether the boy was struck with the bat or was holding the bat when he was struck. While this sort of confusion is a part of the intrinsic ambiguity of human language that becomes the basis for much humor and joke telling, it also has caused destruction and radical cross-cultural misunderstandings.

There is a New Age, liberal equivalent of this deep structure/surface structure dilemma. Both well-meaning New Age liberals and hopeful Indian spiritual traditionalists can easily be swept up into a modern process of imposed cultural change, without recognizing deep structure cultural imposition even when in its midst. The first Indian casualty today in any such New Age spiritual-cultural encounter is most often the strong deep structure cultural value of community and group cohesion that is important to virtually every indigenous people. As adherents of Western cultures, Europeans and Euroamericans live habitual responses to the world that are culturally rooted in an individualist deep structure rather than communitarian. In this "meeting" of cultures, the communal cultural value of Indian people is transformed by those who do not even begin to see the cultural imposition that has occurred, however unintended. Hence, dancing in a ceremony in order "that the people might live" gives way to the New Age, Euroamerican quest for individual spiritual power. What other reason would a New Yorker have for rushing out to South Dakota to spend eight days participating in a Sun Dance ceremony? Yet well-meaning New Agers drive in from New York and Chicago or fly in from Austria and Denmark to participate in annual ceremonies originally intended to secure the well-being of the local, spatially configured community. These visitors see little or nothing at all of the reservation community, pay little attention to the poverty and suffering of the people there, and finally leave having achieved only a personal, individual spiritual high. "That the people might live" survives as merely an abstract ideal at best.

The transformative, coyote twist here involve three things. The first is the impact of white participants on the thinking of younger Indians, many of whom are learning their own ceremonial traditions through increasingly individualist eyes. A second impact is the temptation of many Indians to convert their spiritual tradition into career and economic develop-

Endnotes

1. Francis Paul Prucha, *The Great Father: The United States Government and the American Indian* (Lincoln: Univ. of Nebraska Press, 1984), 2:646f., 800-05; Vine Deloria, Jr. and Clifford M. Lytle, *American Indians, American Justice* (Austin: Univ. of Texas Press, 1983), 230ff. For an example of explicitly articulated federal policy, see Prucha, ed., *Documents of United States Indian Policy* (Lincoln: Univ. of Nebraska Press, 1975), 186ff.

2. Ward Churchill, *Fantasies of the Master Race: Literature, Cinema and the Colonization of American Indians*, ed. M. Annette Jaimes (Boston: South End Press, 1992), 187ff. and 215ff., describes the charlatan-

ment opportunities. A certain wealth can be generated by catering to the individualist needs of white New Age aficionados, and the phenomenon has created a large number of what Churchill calls "plastic" medicine people.[4] The third effect is less immediately perceptible, but just as observable over time. It involves the shift in the thinking of the "traditional" people in an Indian community. Little by little, usually without them even perceiving it, their language about spiritual practices changes both to accommodate the participation of whites and to translate discrete cultural idiosyncrasies for an alien culture in ways that can be more easily understood and appropriated (or rather, misappropriated).

Indian dysfunctionality—a result of the conquest, including the missionary endeavor—means in this case that Indian people are all too ready to participate in our own oppression and continuing conquest. Craving the approval of white acquaintances and hoping for a broader understanding of and appreciation for the validity of traditional ceremonial life, Indian people often rush to invite this new European invasion, the invasion of what remains of tribal ceremonies. I am convinced that this meeting of cultures is in the final analysis harmful to Indian peoples and their tribal traditions. Yet, I would argue that it is equally harmful to those well-meaning white seekers who, having lost themselves back in some white community or white church, hope to find themselves on some Indian reservation. The conquest has always been spiritually harmful to Euroamericans, even when the damage has gone largely unrecognized due to the systemic camouflage of wealth and physical comfort. To their credit, many New Age adherents have seen through this part of the lie, yet they are so systemically ingrained that they fail to recognize their continued participation in acts of conquest.

ism of the likes of Lynn Andrews and Carlos Casteneda with their made-up, pseudo-Indian affectations, as well as the charlatanism of Native American would-be spiritual leaders like Sun Bear and Wallace Black Elk who purport to sell access to Indian ceremonies to non-Indian people. See also Alice B. Kehoe, "Primal Gaia: Primitivists and Plastic Medicine Men," in *The Invented Indian: Cultural Fictions and Government Policies*, ed. James A. Clifton (New Brunswick, N.J.: Transaction Books, 1990), 193-209.

3. Noam Chomsky, *Syntactic Structures*, Janua Linguarum, Series Minor, no. 4 (The Hague: Mouton, 1957); and *Aspects of the Theory of Syntax* (Cambridge, Mass.: MIT Press, 1965).

4. See his essay, "Spiritual Huckterism: The Rise of the Plastic Medicine Men," in Churchill, *Fantasies of the Master Race*, 215-30.

Richard Rodriguez

In this provocative piece Richard Rodriguez, already familiar from his essay earlier in our study, turns our perceptions inside out by suggesting that in an increasingly multicultural America, the new "Native Americans" are receiving today's newcomers with less grace than did the earlier Native Americans who greeted the first immigrants to this continent. Mr. Rodriguez' essay was prepared for Pacific News Service.

We are facing in the United States a moment as epic as that in 1492 when the Indian spied the European galleons on the horizon. In this new pageant of history, the blond becomes the new Native American; the Indian plays the part of the conquistador, the stranger.

Last year, the Census Bureau reported that the nation's foreign-born population is at its highest level since World War II. In California, the state with the greatest number of immigrants, 25 percent of the population is foreign-born.

On the other hand, the United States is the preeminent world power, undisputed cultural force, the inventor, the tongue, the glamour of the world. Should we not expect to be the world's destination? Los Angeles has become the capital of the world, the crossroads city. Rome. Alexandria. London.

Today's new Native Americans do not want anything to do with such a destiny. Polls indicate that a majority of Americans think there are already too many immigrants. Regarding illegal immigrants, particularly, there is even less sympathy.

The irony, of course, is that most of the illegal immigrants, those teenagers who will make a run for it tonight from Tijuana to San Diego, are Indians. We call them Guatemalans or Mexicans, but they are Indians.

In October 1492, the day Columbus arrived, imagining himself to be in the Orient, Indians approached. It is true that from their contact with the European, the tribe of Indians that greeted Columbus would die of the plague. . . . But do not miss the point: the Indian was curious, unafraid of the future.

Today, the new Native Americans in the U.S. seem only afraid of the future. They fuss, complain. A Mexican-American Border Patrolman in San Ysidro whose job it is to protect our sovereign border from the feet of trespassing adolescents, this man complains to me about Mexico—its dust, corruption, poverty. His grandfather fled the Mexican Revolution; now Mexico keeps inching northward.

But the patrolman should understand that borders are two-way affairs. For every incursion by Mexico, the United States has moved southward, transforming the politics of Mexico, the entertainment of Mexico, sending evangelical missionaries exporting pop despair.

Gov. Pete Wilson cheered many of his fellow Californians when he told a Mexican government official to "butt out" of the debate over Proposition 187. I only wonder: Has any American politician ever apologized to Mexico or to Latin America for the way our drug appetite has destabilized our southern neighbors?

Blacks in Watts will tell you that the new immigrants are taking their jobs, raising rents in the neighborhood, transforming Watts from black to brown. The hard truth is that foreign-born blacks from Miami to New York are out-performing the native born.

Peter Brimelow, an Englishman who became a Canadian, then an American, thinks that there are too many immigrants in the United States. And he is more than frank. In his recent book, *Alien Nation*, Mr. Brimelow insists that America is European in its culture and character and must remain so. Asians, meanwhile, are becoming the predominant population at the nine campuses of the University of California.

In New York and Washington, newspapers and networks still speak of a black and white America, the old chessboard. A few blocks from where I live in San Francisco, the Richmond district has filled with Russian and Chinese immigrants. What is the nature of this Sino-Russian meeting?

NBC (or is it ABC?) reports that some percentage of black Americans thinks O.J. is innocent while some other percentage of whites . . . Meanwhile, I wonder what goes on at my neighborhood laundry where Korean owners work alongside their Mexican workers. What sorts of tensions and new understandings are taking place in the new America? . . . In the new America, Guatemalans are singing Lutheran hymns. Blond Native Americans are retiring to Sedona, Arizona, to commune with pre-Columbian spirits.

My barber jets off on a weekend tourist package to Costa Rica. Middle-class tourism makes the once remote world accessible. Businessmen sit in front of the plane headed for Jeddah or Djakarta. . . [and] all over the world peasants are on the move—just like middle-class tourists and businessmen. Do we imagine that we can keep all the peasants of the world under control?

Thai peasants labor in sweat shops in the very center of Los Angeles. It should not surprise us. What was apparent on the TV screen during the 1992 riots was that L.A. had become a third world city. It looked like brown and black Panama City on the screen. If that is shocking to you, then reform the world. Do not expect to live in a world capital isolated from the world.

In the early post-Colombian centuries, the choice given to the Indian was retreat (the reservation model) or engagement with history. In Mexico, the Indian survived by learning Spanish; the Indian even conquered. Spanish is today an Indian language. Mexico has become the linguistic capital of the Spanish-speaking world. . . . The center of Roman Catholicism today is Latin America, not Madrid or Barcelona where the churches are tourist attractions.

Every day there are signs of breakdown. Separate cafeteria tables at the local high school—skins, gays, surfers, Chicanos, etc. Californians blame Chinese immigrants for importing tuberculosis. Skinheads abandon California for Idaho—the new reservation. We are in each other's face. We are on each other's mind.

But everywhere too there are signs of a new world forming. Children are being born in Los Angeles (of two, three, four races) who look exactly like none of their grandparents. They are beautiful children.

By the 18th century, the mixed-race Mexican, the mestizo, had become the predominant population of Mexico, outnumbering the "pure" Indian or European. Mexico, in that way, became the prophetic nation of the Americas. In the United States there was no comparable marriage. To survive, Indians fled to reservations.

Today Hollywood sentimentalizes the dead Indian. Environmentalists have turned the dead Indian into a mascot. Meanwhile, in the new America, Indians from Latin America are having babies and then more babies. This is one of the reasons why the immigrant population is so large: Blond Native Americans are having fewer and fewer children.

It was Jose Vasconcelos, the Mexican philosopher who celebrated the Mexican as "la raza cosmica," the prophetic achievement of the Americas in California. Now it is happening. Africa is meeting Asia. America is discovering the Americas. Indians are trespassing borders. The new Native Americans—blond, black, brown—ponder the future.

Part Four
A BIBLICAL VISION:
FROM DIVERSITY TO PLURALISM

We introduce this part of our study with the words of Dr. Michael Kinnamon of Lexington Theological Seminary, from his introduction to the study paper from which this material was taken.

The dominant reality shaping North American church life in these last years of the twentieth century is surely what Daniel Romero . . . calls "the gift of pluralism." It is not just that people of diverse racial, ethnic, cultural, and religious backgrounds have begun to live in closer proximity—though that is true. And it is not just that our world is becoming more interdependent—though that is also true. The real hallmark of this pluralistic age is that myths by which [European American society has] lived—myths of white or male or American or even Christian superiority—have been exposed for what they are; and this has opened [or forced European Americans] to take the claims of those who see the world through other eyes far more seriously.

Thus I believe that [theologian] Raimundo Panikkar has it right when he declares that "pluralism is the *kairos* of our times," a God-given opportunity to realize new, more inclusive norms of community in both church and society. [Daniel Romero] celebrates the gift of pluralism and the transition it has provoked; but [he] also reminds us that the gift is not without ambiguity and the transition is not without considerable pain. How can we speak of truth given our new appreciation for the diversity of viewpoints? How can we avoid fragmentation in church or society in the absence of a unified vision of the common good? The work done by Dan Romero can help us in facing such questions. [It] also points toward the hard work that still needs to be done.

Daniel F. Romero

Daniel F. Romero is the General Secretary of the Mission Program Unit of the United Church Board for World Ministries. He is an ordained minister of the United Church of Christ, and an attorney.

> In Christ there is no East or West,
> In Him no South or North,
> But one great fellowship of love,
> Throughout the whole wide earth.
> —The Hymnal of the United Church of Christ

How often have we sung those familiar words that boldly declare a universal fellowship in Christ where human barriers have been destroyed and God's people are one? This proclamation reminds us of the global character of the Christian faith. When the Christian community gathers on any Sunday, hymns are sung and scriptures are read in hundreds of languages throughout the world. There is no more moving experience than to join a chorus of distinct voices at a World Council of Churches Assembly reciting the Lord's Prayer in unison in their own languages. A simple prayer binds people to a common history and tradition—a unity that has stood the test of time. Out of this magnificent cultural diversity flow the biblical and theological insights that provide inspiration and challenge. . . .

The life and ministry of Jesus remain the greatest single source of insight into the issues of unity and diversity. Jesus' ministry was one of acceptance and inclusion based on his compassion and remarkable ability to empathize. Empathy is defined as "the projection of one's own personality into the personality of another in order to understand him/her better."[1] The word "empathy" is related to "compassion," the definition of which includes the ability to "feel sorrow, for the sufferings or trouble of another, with the urge to help."[2] Empathy and compassion are particularly important traits for identifying with the needs and concerns of the "other." "Christ reconciles life's opposites," writes feminist African theologian Khumo Nthla,

> rich and poor, master and servant, black and white, male and female. In uniting the most basic pair of opposites, male and female, in his own person and living out the consequences of that fully integrated personality, Jesus has not only shown us the way but has enabled us to integrate all the opposites that conspire to pull us apart, through his Spirit in us.[3]

Jesus' interaction with the Samaritan community provides some insight into the social, cultural, and religious dynamics of his time. Samaria was resettled with various and differing cultural groups after the Babylonian captivity "over several years and under successive (Assyrian) monarchs"[4] (2 Kings 17:24; Ezra 4:10). However, biblical historians have concluded that there were two distinct groupings of people: "The most plausible conclusion is, then, that after the fall of Samaria in 722, the local population consisted of two distinct elements living side by side—a) the remnant of the native Israelites; and (b) the foreign colonists."[5] These groups settled and over time became known as the Samaritans, who, "when they first settled there, did not worship Yahweh" (2 Kings 17:25). However, an attempt was made to teach the Samaritans how and whom to worship. The scriptures record that they did worship Yahweh but "also served their own gods," continuing practices that were unacceptable to the people of Israel (2 Kings 17:33). The conflict between the Samaritans and the Jews "is wholly and most naturally explicable as a continuance of the inveterate hostility between Israel and Judah . . . but reached its culmination in the erection by the [Samaritans] of their own distinctive temple on Mount Gerizim."[6] The place of worship, Mount Gerizim versus Mount Zion in Jerusalem, became the chief source of rivalry between the two groups.[7]

Jesus had grown up with the Jewish view of the Samaritans, a view that regarded them "at best, as one degree nearer than Gentiles, but still not as full-fledged members of the house of Israel."[8] They were a group with mixed religious practices. They worshiped the God of Israel but never gave up "serving" other gods. In short, they were different. The two communities, Israel and Samaria, had very little contact with each other. The Samaritans were often referred to as "foreigners," even though they traced their ancestry to the very same source as the Jews. Labeling a group as "foreign" or "alien" builds walls and strips people of their identity and their humanity.

In a dramatic break with custom, tradition, and cultural taboos, Jesus transcended the barriers of separation and reached out to the Samaritans as individuals and as a community. In exchange, the Samaritans often responded with respect and affection. The most instructive example we have of an attempt by Jesus to reach out to the Samaritans was his conversation with the woman at Jacob's well as recorded in John 4. This encounter at the well has become particularly meaningful, for Jesus not only drank with a Samaritan but with a Samaritan *woman*. Jesus and the woman discussed the contentious issue of Samaritan worship practices. He confronted her about her personal life, much to the astonishment of the disciples. So shocked were they that they did not even question him about it. After hearing the woman's testimony, many in her community became curious and invited Jesus into their homes. He responded by spending time with them and sharing his faith—a faith they later adopted as their own, proclaiming him Savior of the world. Jesus became a bridge between these two communities.

The Gospel of Luke also records experiences and events with the Samaritan community. In Luke 9:52–53, Jesus is not received by Samaritan villagers on his way to Jerusalem. It could very well be that the messengers Jesus sent to make ready for his arrival did not share the sensitivities Jesus had developed toward the Samaritan community. So put out were the disciples that they wanted "to command fire to come down from heaven and consume them [the Samaritans]" (Luke 9:54). It was such an outrageous suggestion that Jesus "rebuked them." This is often our response to persons who do not share our customs and cultural background: a desire to destroy them. But Jesus would have nothing to do with these genocidal tendencies.

There are very few people who are not familiar with the story of the good Samaritan. Even our civil laws have so-called good Samaritan statutes and ordinances that protect those who attempt to rescue others. It was the Samaritan, the outcast, the unacceptable one, whom Jesus used as an example to others of the meaning of eternal life (Luke 10:25–37). In Luke's story of Jesus' healing of the ten lepers, the Samaritan is the only one of the ten who thanks Jesus: "Were not ten made clean? But the other nine, where are they? Was none of them found to return and give praise to God except this foreigner?" Then he said to him, "Get up and go on your way; your faith has made you well" (Luke 17:17).

Jesus reached out to the suspect Samaritan community because he believed that all people were children of God. God's unconditional love was available to all, and Jesus knew that those barriers constructed by humans were not God's barriers. Jesus exhibited patience, and above all else, he listened to those who did not share his history, whether they were Samaritans, tax collectors, or prostitutes. He asked penetrating questions of the woman at the well but he did not demean her because of her beliefs. Rather, he laid out an expectation that one day all would worship God in spirit and truth. There was a clear invitation that she be among them. The fact that she was a woman who bore witness to him among her own people was revolutionary.

The apostle Paul's and disciple Peter's differing approaches to ministry are further examples of diversity within the early Christian community. In the midst of the conflict between Peter and Paul regarding who would be admitted to the community of the faithful and how, Paul produced powerful images of unity and oneness. It was in the context of Paul's understanding of Christ's mission that he sought unity. Paul was vehemently opposed to separation on the basis of race, social status, and gender: "There is no longer Jew or Greek, there is no longer slave or free, there is no longer male and female; for all of you are one in Christ Jesus" (Gal. 3:28). Paul was troubled by Peter's refusal to eat with Gentile converts (Gal. 2:11–21), and the intensity of his passion about this blatant act of separation is hard to miss. Paul strongly defended acceptance on the basis of justification by faith, not works (Gal. 2:1–17). David Bosch speaks of a new kind of body:

> God in Christ has accepted us unconditionally; we have to do likewise with regard to one another. On the basis of Paul's thinking, it is inconceivable that, in a given locality, converts could comprise two congregations—one Torah observant Jewish Christians, and another of non-observant Gentile Christians. In the death and resurrection of Jesus Christ a new age has dawned, in which Jew and Gentile are joined together without distinction in the one people of God. . . . And Christ's work of reconciliation does not bring two parties into the same room that they may settle their differences; it leads to a new kind of body in which human relations are being transformed.[9]

That "new kind of body in which human relations are being transformed" has become the centerpiece of Christians' understanding of unity amid diversity. Paul's elaborate description in 1 Corinthians 12 of the body of Christ has left us with an important image for the vision of pluralism as a gift of God. God works through the Holy Spirit to bring people together in one body.

Endnotes

1. *Webster's New World Dictionary*, 3d ed.
2. Ibid.
3. Khumo Nthla, "Life in Abundance—for Women Too?" *Challenge* (Institute of Contextual Theology, South Africa, August 1992): 11.
4. Buttrick and Harmon, eds., *The Interpreter's Bible*, vol. IV (Nashville: Abingdon-Cokesbury Press, 1962), 191.
5. Ibid. 192.
6. Ibid.
7. Ibid., 193–94
8. Ibid., 191.
9. Bosch, 167–68.

Part Five
BARRIERS AMONG US AND WITHIN OURSELVES: ETHICAL ISSUES OF LIFE IN A MULTICULTURAL SOCIETY

In a previous essay, Peggy McIntosh examined her life as a European American woman of privilege, and contrasted it with what she perceived to be the problems she would encounter as an African American woman in similar circumstances. The essay focused directly on the need for persons of the majority culture to examine their lives, their societies, and their institutions, and be prepared to make real choices—real changes—so that those in the society of other racial/ethnic strains might be regarded and treated in ways that persons of European American ancestry take largely for granted.

The following essay by Anne Bathurst Gilson and Barbara A. Weaver continues to examine these issues. It is a piece aimed at readers who are part of the majority culture, and poses the kinds of ethical issues and choices that dare no longer be avoided: not only because faithfulness to a Christian understanding of God's people demands it, but also because in the most pragmatic of ways, a multicultural society is unworkable without it. Weaver and Gilson dwell on the beauty of diversity, but, perhaps more importantly for our study, they point out exactly how and why European Americans need to reach out and change their often insular and exclusionary behavior. If they have not yet done so, it is time to begin; if they are already on that path, they will have discovered a new breadth and richness in the scope of their personal relationships. Most importantly, they will have learned that the journey toward justice and inclusion for all people in our society begins with the actions of those who have the influence, the courage, the will, and the faith to risk shaking the foundations of their own churches, communities, and homes.

Anne Bathurst Gilson and Barbara A. Weaver

Watch your step. The patio tiles are still a bit damp from the dew. Look over there. There—in the middle of the patio floor. Over there. Try shielding your eyes from the bright morning sun. Look there. Isn't that mosaic incredible? Look at the brilliant colors—at the remarkable shading. The sunshine splashing on the distinct edges of the pieces makes the light dance. What an amazing visual feast! Such careful crafting—each piece so beautifully different in itself—and yet fit together so artistically. Can we linger for a while longer? I want to take in the richness of this mosaic, to absorb the colors and textures. I want to feel the subtle, yet bold, qualities that carry me into such a vastly different and wonderful world.

Close your eyes for just a moment. Take in the shades, the textures and shapes of this mosaic. Take a deep breath. Slowly open your eyes and begin to take in the vision of each other. Look around you—at our various shades, textures and shapes. Feel the complexity of our diverse heritage. Can you hear the life-giving power of African American spirituals? Can you taste the Eucharist with rice and papaya juice? Can you hear the prayers for rain as corn and soybean crops wither in the blazing sun?

Anne Bathurst Gilson is a Visiting Scholar at Episcopal Divinity School, Cambridge, Massachusetts. Barbara A. Weaver, a former Assistant General Secretary for the Women's Division, Board of Global Ministries, United Methodist Church, is a doctoral student in education at Boston College.

What would our communities of faith be like if we celebrated our differences? What if our communities had both respectful separation for different groups and respectful coming together? What if we decided that our multicultural communities were of such importance that we learned each other's music, not just the tunes, but the history, and the feelings of singing today and yesterday . . . not only music of the church, but music that comes from people's movements?

What if we decided that our multicultural communities were of such importance that we learned each other's stories, not beginning with questions, but with active listening . . . hearing what has been written in history, how it has been written, and what has not been written and asking why . . . feeling each other's stories with our bodies and souls?

What if we decided that our multicultural communities were of such importance that we learned each other's languages, maybe in formal course work or maybe asking what is the word for this or that, what are usual greetings or expressions of politeness? What if we became more attentive to cultural differences of expressions and ways of being?

What if we decided that our multicultural communities were of such importance that we learned about each others' images of God? What if we opened ourselves to images of God as an old Black man or woman, or an old Asian man or woman, or a very young Native American person, or a campesino from Mexico? What if we stretched ourselves and learned each other's interpretations of Bible stories?

What if the dominant group in our communities really welcomed all to the table and embraced the sharing of power and control?

We invite you, the reader, to struggle with us in aligning our formal faith proclamations with our day-to-day theology and practice.

Our society is a multi-color, multi-dimensional mosaic in a patio of sameness. We know so much about sameness. The North American society sings to us, talks to us, screams at us, points out to us, demands from us to look basically the same, act basically the same, feel basically the same. We are encouraged to buy acceptance, respect, and love through sameness.

This emphasis on needing to be the same is strongly rooted in American history. Calvin Stowe, writing in 1836, maintained that "there must be a national feeling, a national assimilation. . . . It is altogether essential to our national strength and peace that the foreigners should cease to be Europeans and become Americans."[1] At commencement exercises at the Ford English School in 1916, graduates participating in a ritual of citizenship "dressed in traditional national costumes, disembarked from an immigrant ship and disappeared into a gigantic melting pot." After their teachers stirred the pot, the graduates re-emerged, garbed in "American" clothing and enthusiastically waving flags.[2] A decade later, sociologist

Henry Pratt Fairchild wrote that unrestricted immigration, undergirded by the melting-pot philosophy, was "slowly, insidiously, irresistibly eating away the very heart of the United States"—a heart that was based on the culture of those early arrivals to its shores, namely those of English, Irish, German, and Scandinavian stock.[3] A need for sameness was clearly and thoroughly integrated into an understanding of U.S. culture.

Today, there is no denying it. Our churches—as well as the wider society in which we live—are becoming living mosaics of differences. As Christians, we publicly state our commitment to people of all races and cultures as we read the scriptures, pray, sing, and proclaim together. In Paul's day, he described this rich community mosaic as a body.

> Just as each of our bodies has several parts and each part has a separate function, so all of us, in union with Christ, form one body and as parts of it we belong to each other. (Romans 12:4-6)

Our communities, like the communities of our early church, are called over and over again to faithfulness. We say in our creeds that we are one people united in Christ. We proclaim one God, Creator and Sustainer of us all. We write policies and invoke doctrines that keep an inclusive vision before us. Formally, we proclaim we are "in union with Christ and that we form one body and, as parts of that body, we belong to each other."

Such is our formal theology. But what of our day-to-day theology, our practice? How do we actually live our daily lives—both as a community of faith and as individuals? How do we make decisions? If we are honest, our practice, our day-to-day theology, does not always reflect the formal theological pronouncements we publicly profess.

In the history of Christianity, when we have not known what to do with the differences between us, they have been systematically labelled "pagan" or "heathen" and have been destroyed. We have referred to those who are different alternatively as "heathen," or as "children" or as "non-human." We have sexually exploited what we find appealing in difference, and have done away with what is unappealing. At times, we have done both. Womanist ethicist, Joan M. Martin rightly states that when we take seriously the fact that we are made in the image of God, then we take the differences between us seriously. She further maintains that if we fail to recognize and value difference as part of what makes up creation, then we cannot clailm to be ethical people. "We can either make difference that which kills us, or that which enlivens us. It's as simple as that."[4]

Much of the intolerance for those who differ from the white, Euro-American, male norm has historically been undergirded by Christian theology and is evident in the rhetoric emanating from the mouths of contemporary right-wing hate groups. This questionable theological inheritance has deep roots. Winthrop D. Jordan, writing on American attitudes toward Black people from the sixteenth through the nineteenth centuries, insists that in the seventeenth century *difference* was "the indispensable key to the degradation of Negroes in English America."[5] Being a Christian was associated with being white, free, and English. The "heathen condition of the Negroes seemed of considerable importance to English settlers . . . heathenism was associated in some settlers' minds with the condition of slavery."[6] This emphasis on heathenism occurred because settlers, insecure in their ability to reproduce the institutions and practices of English Christianity, felt a need to focus on those who were so obviously defective in terms of adherence to Christian practices. In understanding how slavery was justified in the minds of captors, it is clear how Black people were distanced—by the labels of heathen or unchristian (read: non-human), and thus exploited and often destroyed.

Hence, race, and now multiculturalism, are life or death issues. The matter before us is urgent and cannot be relegated to simply a short study on the issue. For many people, dealing with issues of living in a multicultural society is *not* an option. It is part of who they are. Treating multiculturalism as a passing fad is the privilege of those who identify with white privilege. Those of us who have white privilege, who are white *and* Euro-American, have the luxury of choosing when to engage the issues of multiculturalism. We have the power that comes from being part of the norm.

Why, you might ask, concern ourselves with the mess that has been made of human relationships? Would it not be better to focus on our spiritual development as Christians instead of mucking around in the conflict-ridden issues of the differences between us—of race, class and culture? We believe that, as Christians, our spirituality is very much connected with the challenges of the world and that the Kingdom of God is already among us. As Jesus embraced differences in his ministry (see, for example, his encounter with the Samaritan woman in John 4:9), indeed, as Jesus embodied difference from the cultural expectations of his day, so too are we who call ourselves Christians to go forth into the world.

We are two white, Euro-American, middle-class women who have lived our lives connected to mainline Protestant denominations, and we approach the ethical issues of multiculturalism from a foundation of Christian faith. We understand that we have privilege by virtue of our race, class, and culture. We see also that we are responsible for using that privilege to confront the structures that perpetuate oppression on the basis of race, class, and culture. Indeed, as Christians, we believe this to be a central part of our faith commitment.

We invite other white people to join us in exploring strategies to truly share power. We are posing the difficult question: Are we truly committed to multiculturalism, or are we really only welcoming to "honorary whites" (read: those who give up their cultural differences)? It is time, past time, to be raising this question. We simply must look racism in the face and begin—or continue—to deepen our analysis of anti-racist behavior. We believe that we must look for the gaps between the theology we formally profess and our theological practice—or day-to-day living out of our faith. How does our understanding of God inform our living ethically in a multicultural society?

Multiculturalism and Social Construction Theory

Before progressing too much further, it is important to be clear what we mean by the term "multiculturalism." In this chapter, we use the term "multiculturalism" in two basic senses. First and foremost, human existence is multicultural—however resistant humanity may be to acknowledging it. Jaime Wurzel explains that this resistance probably comes from "the survival imperative of the ethnocentric impulse." Emphasizing sameness has been seen as a surer—and easier—path to survival than has recognizing and living with the differences between us.[7]

The second sense in which we use the term "multiculturalism" has to do with multiculturalism as a set of principles, a perspective, which guides peoples' actions in a multicultural context. While these principles can be learned, the key to a multicultural perspective is a fundamental awareness of difference. Wurzel notes that since the impulse to ethnocentrism is very deeply interconnected with both unconscious and cultural behaviors, most people have in-built resistances to viewing society as multiculture. He asserts that one must first "become aware of one's own ethnocentric conditioning and [then] accept the fact that society is indeed multicultural."[8]

Our understandings of God, culture, humanity, and the positive or negative *meanings* that are given to the various differences between us are shaped or constructed in the context of our particular web of "social relationships." They are not fixed in stone, but rather are influenced by and influence our particular relationships. This is the primary assumption from which we approach the subject of multiculturalism and is formally known as the theory of social construction. Joan M. Martin says social construction theory allows her to keep her faith rooted in the realities of this world. For her, spiritual realities are rooted in every-day life.[9]

Social construction theory says we not only give meaning to the relationships between us as people, animals, God, and the earth, we also structure them, embedding meanings of power in them, thus shaping the way we act in our families, and through religions; economic and social forces; community norms, mores and regulations; and political agendas and policies. In theological language, "the freedom we have been given to make the world around us is . . . so all-consuming, so confidently given to us by God, that we have the freedom to create that which is of ourselves."[10] When you understand that oppressive ideas about race, gender, and class are constructed by people, you realize they can be deconstructed. Social construction theory requires us to seek out, listen, to, and act upon the concerns of people from various perspectives of racial, economic, gender, and cultural experience to learn how difference has been used to construct both superior and inferior social positions. Beyond the deconstruction of oppression, we are free to construct ideas about appreciating the differences between us as gifts, rather than approaching the reality of our differences as a "problem."[11]

A contemporary distancing tactic, described by Anne Marie Hunter and John Raines, is the phenomenon of enforced visibility. This involves being directly watched (standing out because of visual difference). Hunter and Raines characterize the power, pervasiveness, and invasiveness of what is considered normal, usual, or common as a "social" or "normative gaze" which "controls and conditions . . . behaviors, speech patterns, body movements, world views, and world understandings."[12] In a room where there are only a few people of color, the white people in the room can usually describe what the people of color wore, how they sat, what they said or did not say. However, more often than not, those same white people cannot recall what other white people wore, how they sat, or what they did or did not say. Frequently, when a person of color is described, an adjective is used: "the intelligent Black lawyer" or "the capable Native American teacher." Although these descriptions are meant to be complimentary, in actuality they denote that these people are the exceptions, are a "credit to their race," and that most people who are not white cannot measure up.

Hunter and Raines believe that "seeing and being seen is a socially constructed activity in which as a self-in-relationship, we are constantly being formulated and reformulated." Furthermore, they point out that the process of seeing and being seen is difficult to avoid since it is undergirded "by economic and social systems that have the power to reward or to punish. . . . The gaze is internalized by those who are watched . . . the monitored learn to monitor themselves."[13] Thus, the distance between us is reinforced.

Attitudinal Barriers to Multiculturalism

It seems to us that two of the primary factors involved in maintaining difference as that which must be distanced, exploited, and/or destroyed are fear and the need to control. These two factors are deeply entwined: if I am operating from a fear-based mentality, then I am more likely to seek to control that of which I am afraid by distancing it, exploiting it, or destroying it. And, conversely, at the suggestion that those who are being controlled might be capable of knowing what is in their own best interests, those who have been in control clench the reins of control even more tightly, fearing the specter of change and the unknown and what it might mean for their own power. From a position of privilege, fear functions as a way of closing one off from challenges; it represents change and possible losses of power.

It was fear of the unfamiliar that led Anne's sister to warn her not to travel to Central America, because those people "are savages and live in bamboo huts." It is fear and the need to be in control that has spurred on those championing the "only English shall be spoken" language movement. It is the need for pat answers, for so-called security, and for control of the shape of reality that leads some to view history as merely a collection of facts, rather than as a perspective that is socially constructed. And it is fear of others' need to control that lead an African American woman colleague of Barbara's to caution her teenaged son to be careful about what he does in public because his race makes him a "natural" suspect: many store owners would assume that he is stealing something.

The perpetuation of racism, classism, and disdain for other cultural perspectives helps white, Euro-American, middle-class people maintain the status quo and feel a sense of security (however fleeting it may be) and of being in control in a world/church with very little security and increasingly few arenas that can be controlled. Fear-based control is what too many have based their lives on. Without it, it is feared that things will fall apart. Not to be in control is perceived as a threat to the family, the nation, the church—even to Christianity itself. Many have argued that not maintaining control—over those who are perceived to need our protection, over the dominance of the English language, over who is welcome at our tables—is a threat to civilization. It is sometimes even argued that Christianity demands that we stay in control!

Control—and the fear it is based on—is often disguised as protection of others. In this scenario, the one who is different is infantilized or demonized, and is therefore to be protected or is someone from whom others should be protected. Either way, the one who is different is distanced and exploited and, at times, destroyed. Thus it is that an "us versus them" mentality holds sway which is reinforced by legal, economic, cultural, and religious systems invoking "ethics," the name of God, and the good of the country. And violence against those who are different is even sometimes defended as being God's will. Because this violence is interpreted as being divinely sanctioned (and/or nationally sanctioned), the illusion of maintaining control is sustained.

Ethical Principles of Action for Furthering the End of White Privilege, White Racism, and White Supremacy

We need to take time to reflect on the gaps between what we believe and what we do. When we connect both our formal, professed theology and our day-to-day lived theology/practice, when we truly respect the differences between us, when we "form one body and as parts of it belong to each other," then our mosaic survives and thrives. As a beginning point in the ongoing process of filling in the gaps between believing and doing, we suggest the following principles of action.[14]

We need to value our nagging suspicions and continually hold the status quo suspect. We need to question what has been deemed unquestionable by those who have a vested interest in distancing, exploiting, and destroying those who are different from the white, middle-class, euro-american norm. We need to raise such questions as . . . Why, when Barbara was Christmas shopping for an eight-year-old African American girl, could she only find dark-skinned dolls with white features? Who has what to gain by maintaining the distances between us? Why not approach history as a collection of many stories told from many different perspectives? What is it about the differences between us that leads well-meaning parents to remark that "I have many friends who are Jewish (or African American or Asian, and so on), but I wouldn't want my daughter or son to marry one . . ."? What would happen if we opened our ears to really hear one another? Would the walls come tumbling down?

The principle of suspicion means that we must begin to question and dismantle the various myths we have held about race, class, and culture. For those of us who hold white, Euro-American privilege, we need to understand that our unearned privilege matters greatly if we are to put into action our Christian faith. We need to find constructive ways to balance it and ask questions about how it functions to keep others at a distance. Once we have begun to question, it is well-nigh impossible to turn back the clock of awareness. Some things will never again be the same.

Another principle has to do with the details of the differences between us. We must speak honestly of the particularities of our lives and actively listen to others speak honestly of their lives. We must push open the question of what is "normal," and what is considered "normative." Paying attention to the particularities of our lives—what it means to live in the midst of all our differences—helps open us up to new ways of seeing reality. When we hear and share stories about what it is like to live as an African American woman in a racist and sexist world/church, as a working-class white woman in a classist and sexist world/church, as an Arab man in a world/church that associates whiteness with being Euro-American, or as a Jewish woman in a country that too many consider to be a "Christian country," the hold of isolation and alienation on our lives is loosened and new possibilities and connections can emerge.

Taking seriously the particularities of our lives, the differences between us, must mean that no one particularity should ever be considered normative. The aim is not for sameness. Rather, difference is approached as a gift, an opportunity to change. The differences between us—of race, gender, sexual orientation, age, class, religion, nationality, physical and mental abilities—as well as those particularities we hold in common, matter deeply because they make us who we are. What is claimed as being morally normative then becomes not a matter of sameness, but rather becomes a question of that which enhances or detracts from our well-being and that of others and provides opportunities for us to grow. We can never go back to seeing the differences between us as a danger.

Another principle is that of self-knowing, of coming to understand, in the context of community, one's power-in-relation.[15] Self-knowing is about understanding that one has the power to say no to oppression and injustice. Self-knowing is about understanding how one's actions affect others. If one does not know oneself, one's relations to others and God are unrooted. Self-knowing empowers all who have been relegated to the margins of the world/church to say no to others' perceptions of who they should be.

Yet another principle, one connected to self-knowing, concerns self-loving. This is central to the gospel imperative to love our neighbors as our selves. (Matthew 22:34-40; James 2:1-9) If we do not love ourselves, our capacity to love another is damaged. Self-loving requires that a resounding no be said to those self-destructive impulses that in reality do not come from the self, but rather are rooted in a racist, sexist, and classist church/world order. Self-loving means that we need to work together to resist ongoing victimization, finding ways to *survive* together and perhaps even *thrive* together. Self-loving also requires of us that we utter a resounding yes to our right to exist and our capacity to act as moral agents in the world.

Loving our neighbors as our selves continues the gospel imperative and is a principle of action that combines explicit self-loving with an equally explicit neighbor-loving and challenges the mind-set that would keep us distancing, exploiting, and destroying those who are different from us. With a love of neighbor as self, we are more able to embrace our differences, to see them as gifts to be lifted up among us rather than as threat. With a combined love of self and neighbor, the fear that has fed into the need to control (and thus distance, exploit, and destroy) the differences between us can be transformed into energy for authentic engagement with one another. The gospel-rooted love of neighbor as self can generate both individual and collective transformation.

Another principle of action is that of being intentional about re-connecting ourselves. A dynamic of alienation and disconnection has pervaded many of our lives, leaving us lonely and in pain, with pieces of our lives cordoned off, one from the other. We are alienated from intimately knowing ourselves, one another, and certainly those who are different from us. When we re-connect, we can help each other move through fear together. We learn to keep our lines of communication open and make a commitment to overcome disconnection.

By re-connecting, we become ever more aware of how our beautiful mosaic of differences can be damaged by habitual, yet violating phrases like "black-balled from a club" or "the black sheep of the family" or "Indian giver" or "non-white." The mosaic can be damaged by using color symbolism such as white as positive and good; black as negative and evil. So too must we re-evaluate such terms as "culturally deprived" and "culturally disadvantaged." What these terms actually mean is that those to whom they refer lack the cultural background of the controlling structure; the suggestion is that their own culture is not the right culture. Likewise, the terms "culturally different" and "culturally distinct" imply that one is out of step with the dominant culture. And the familiar U.S. usage of the term "melting pot" functions to melt away other cultures through acculturation and assimilation. Those not acculturated or assimilated—historically African Americans and Native Americans—have been distanced and destroyed, through lynching and being relegated to reservations, respectively. Our multi-faceted mosaic has also been damaged by using words from a particular historical time that distort what happened—for example, "the master bedded his slave" denies the radical evil of slavery. "The white captor raped an African woman held in captivity" gets closer to the profound violation that occurred. These language issues are symptomatic of a widespread ethnocentrism that has functioned as a barrier to the acceptance and celebration of multiculturalism on both an individual and an institutional level.

Revisiting Paul's imagery again, the body is hurt by blatant as well as subtle dismissals of its parts. Racism is a continuing wounding of the body; it can be compared to saying to a leg, or elbow, or head, or voice: "We don't need you." Our community bodies have parts crushed by the insistence of those who hold power that a particular way of working, praying, singing, loving, leading, or describing God is superior and thus the only way. In re-connecting, the details of our lives can be affirmed within our sameness, within the friction born of our differences.

Finally, solidarity must be considered as central to the consideration of ethics in a multicultural society. We need to ask who is excluded from our mosaic? Who is included? Can it be easily added to? And how? Solidarity means that those with class, gender, cultural, and white privilege must examine that privilege. Accountability is critical to solidarity and it entails a willingness to risk, to confront one another (which sometimes happens when lines of communication are open) and to disagree. It means not being afraid to risk what is a false unity. It means discarding the need for sameness. And it also means not accepting premature overtures of reconciliation when the demands of justice have not been satisfied.

Solidarity means that those of us who have had privilege can no longer be "one of the silent ones," the well-intended who become invisible, who disappear when a racial situation gets tough. So often, those of us who are white Euro-Americans have remained silent in situations of racial conflict because we have feared alienating our white colleagues by speaking up. We need to be clear about where we stand. We need to risk speaking up. And sometimes we even need to risk being wrong. Solidarity means that we risk new relationships and growth.

When we look together at all the various differences in our communities, we are again reminded about Paul's message to the church in Rome. As a toe, we cannot say to the heart or to the Kim family, we can do

Endnotes

1. As quoted in D. Tyeck, *Turning Points in American Educational History* (Waltham, Mass.: Blaisdell, 1967).
2. American Social History Project, *Who Built America? Working People and the Nation's Economy, Politics, Culture, and Society*, Vol. 2 (New York: Pantheon Books, 1992) 256.
3. H. P. Fairchild, *The Melting Pot Mistake* (Boston: Little, Brown, 1926) 261.
4. Joan M. Martin, presentation at Living Values 2 Consultation at the Scarritt-Bennett Center in Nashville, Tennessee, January 1993, 10-11.
5. Winthrop D. Jordan, *White Over Black: American Attitudes Toward the Negro, 1550-1812* (New York: W.W. Norton & Company, 1968) 91.
6. Ibid. See also John C. Hurd, *The Law of Freedom and Bondage in the United States*, 2 volumes (Boston, 1858-62), I, 159-60. 7. Jaime S. Wurzel, "Multiculturalism and Multicultural Education" in *Toward Multiculturalism: A Reader in Multicultural Education* (Yarmouth, Maine: Intercultural Press, Inc., 1988) 1.
8. Ibid.
9. Joan M. Martin, Ibid.
10. Joan M. Martin, Ibid. See also Anne Bathurst Gilson, *Eros Breaking Free: Interpreting Sexual Theo-Ethics* (Cleveland: The Pilgrim Press, 1995), 8-9.
11. Conversation with Ann Craig, October 1995.
12. Anne Marie Hunter and John Raines, "Power and the Gendered Gaze," an unpublished paper presented at the 1993 Annual Meeting of the American Academy of Religion, 1-2.
13. Hunter and Raines, 2.
14. These principles are adapted from an earlier article. See Gilson, "Family

Values Versus Valuing Families of Choice" in *The Journal of Feminist Studies in Religion* (Spring 1996).

15. For more on "power-in-relation" see Carter Heyward, *The Redemption of God* (Lanham, MD: University Press of America, 1982).

without you. Or to the ears, Mr. Johnson, we can do without you. Or to the lungs, Ms. Patterson, we can do without you. As a toe, we can say to the other body parts: It is amazing that you do what you do. We respect you. We cannot do what you do. But, together, we can work in ways that celebrate our differences.

Feel the wonder of our mysterious mosaic, of our differences.

As Paul wrote, "Just as each of our bodies has several parts and each part has a separate function, so all of us, in union with Christ, *form one body and as parts of it we belong to each other.*" (Romans 12:4-6)

Part Six
STRIVING TOWARD A MULTICULTURAL CHURCH

In this final section of our study we examine what is happening in actual congregations engaged in multicultural ministry. We present conversations with members and the pastor of First Church of Christ, Hartford, Connecticut; a conversation with Pastor Ruth S. Morales, associate pastor at First Baptist Church, Los Angeles, California; and an essay by Inez Fleming, an African American member of the multiracial Oakhurst Presbyterian Church in Decatur, Georgia. Issues addressed repeatedly by all three congregations, and seen as crucial in a meaningful multiracial ministry, are those of power sharing and decision making in a manner that includes and takes seriously individuals from all groups—not just the majority culture.

We continue with selected passages from an essay by David Ng. It is an important look at Christian ministry and education through the lens of a Chinese-American theologian who speaks, also, for the larger Asian community. We conclude this section, and our study, with a poignant essay by Joyce Carlson, a Christian educator and writer of mixed Aboriginal–European Canadian background, who discusses the critical role of language in cross-cultural communication generally, and in the church, specifically.

First Church of Christ
Hartford, Connecticut

The First Church of Christ in Hartford has been an active congregation since 1632. Its members first covenanted in Cambridge, but, as dissenters, they moved into the wilderness in 1636 to found the frontier community of Hartford, Connecticut. Today the urban setting of First Church is both inspiring and discouraging. In a region suffering from major losses in the aerospace and insurance industries, Hartford's Main Street is generally quiet except for special celebrations. On a typical Sunday morning it looks like an unused movie set—attractive buildings without people. First Church, commonly known as Center Church, stands alone on the west side of Main. Its front is marked by tall white columns and a three-tiered steeple. An ancient burial ground extends behind the church. It seems the classic New England church. True to Puritan roots, even the Christian cross is absent to avoid any semblance of idolatry. In this historic setting, Center Church is engaged in a new kind of ministry—yet one very much in character with its adventurous and principled Puritan past. [Adapted from "Congregating: Center Church" by Carl S. Dudley, **The Christian Century,** *October 26, 1994.]*

[The following conversation was held at Center Church in August 1995. It is instructive to note that the multiethnic membership of Center Church is overwhelmingly professional and well-educated. Present were Mark Welch, European American; Beverly Morgan-Welch, African American and spouse of Mark; Hugh Penney, European American, retired pastor; Gladys Hernandez, Puerto Rican; Leslie Thompson, European American, married to an African American; and the interviewer, Anne Leo Ellis. Center Church's pastor, the Reverend J. Alan McLean, was on vacation at the time of the interview. Two other members, Robin Roy and Larry Roeming, both European American, talked with the interviewer later that same day. The Reverend McLean's comments were made by telephone.]

MARK WELCH: This congregation is probably as well-intentioned and focused in its efforts to create a hospitable environment for diverse participation as any congregation I've known. The leadership is committed to this goal, and we try to live that out. But, there are still barriers to its realization, particularly concerning issues of power-sharing.

GLADYS HERNANDEZ: I think the multicultural emphasis began when the number of members began to decrease; when the economy got tight; when funds were not coming in. Adversity is a good way to stimulate change. We began to think of all those unchurched people out there. But those unchurched people were Puerto Rican and African American. African Americans have many wonderful churches on the North End. But now as they and Puerto Ricans begin to move west and south, we need to bring them in.

Do they want to be brought in?

HERNANDEZ: Some do. Some of them have said, "We've lived all our lives in Hartford and never knew this was a church." And they wouldn't have *dared* to come in the doors. I think our attitude has changed. I have no complaints about the way *I* was treated. I've been here forty-one years, and I've never felt discriminated against. I was brought in and I participated, and have continued to do that. To my knowledge I was the first. It's going to be a tough climb, and we won't have thousands at our door. Currently the church has approximately a dozen Hispanic members. There are probably about a dozen African American members. A number of these are interracially married.

LESLIE THOMPSON: My husband is black, and we were looking for a church we would feel comfortable in. He visited the *very* white church I had grown up in, and the first time I brought him there he was stared at, which was mortifying to me. By contrast, Center Church has a very comfortable atmosphere.

WELCH: I think this is a great church, and probably unique for the reasons Leslie cited. I was serving a small black church, and when Beverly and I came here, we looked for more than a year to find a church in which we had a modicum of comfort.

BEVERLY MORGAN-WELCH: We would go to churches where I would be asked if I could be helped. I would walk through the door when the service was starting, and almost universally I was stopped; I was *not* welcomed, and so we'd sit down for an hour, and I'd say, "No way!"

WELCH: We went to one church on a very crowded Sunday, but no one was listening to the service; everyone was craning their necks watching us.

MORGAN-WELCH: I grew up in a small interracial church in Connecticut, and have been a member of the United Church of Christ all of my life, so this was not an unfamiliar setting. A number of things are interesting about this church, and when you walk in the door, you are welcomed. It was a huge relief when we sat down, and I said to Mark, "This is it!"

WELCH: We had already talked to the pastor, and he was embracing and inviting.

THOMPSON: That's a big advantage of the church. It's just overwhelmingly friendly—as far as I know, to everyone. In a lot of churches they'll hand you a program, and no one will talk to you.

How do the older, more established members of Center Church view these changes?

MORGAN-WELCH: There are people here who have been members for fifty years or more, who are open and embracing. I was on the diaconate shortly after becoming a member, and I ran the Christmas potluck supper [at the church's senior residence] for maybe five years. I had no sense that people thought it strange I should be there. Nor were they asking me [the kinds of inappropriate questions I field every day of my life], for example, "So . . . have you been to college?" Not to have this was like, "Yes! This is good." Instead, I'm asked, "Where do you live? What brought you here? Are you coming back?" These questions say to me, "I like you being here. Are you coming back? We'd all like you to be here." People are friendly in a deliberate but casual way, rather than "Aha! I've spied you, and I'm coming your way because I'm afraid no one's going to make you welcome." In such an environment, if somebody disagrees with you or gets angry with you, you are free to decide whether it's because of your color or whether it's political, and then make a determination whether or not you want to respond.

What do you think this has done for those people in the congregation who are European American?

WELCH: I think some of them have grown.

HERNANDEZ: I think they've grown in acceptance. I remember there were certain people I had pigeonholed into "They'll never accept me whole-heartedly; I will never visit them; my children will never play with their children; they'd never ask me." But once, when I was up in Maine, they greeted us like we were old friends. And I thought, Aha! They're begin-ning to understand that people are different but not so different. That you open doors, and discover each other. They were so lovely! I felt ashamed of myself because I was the one who had pigeonholed. And I'm thinking not only of myself, but of other people coming into the church. This church has always welcomed diversity, because many of the groups that came here, Germans, Armenians, Italians, were welcomed in earlier days.

THOMPSON: When we first came here, everybody was welcome. We were brought right into the power structure. I soon became co-deacon, and my husband became moderator. There was no cutting people out. That's be-cause the number of new people was fairly small. But when it came down to making decisions, the congregation did not go through a process— which we now do. The first issue that I remember—and I remember it as painful (not so much because of the outcome but because of the way it was done)—was whether our senior minister and our associate minister should be co-pastors. This was brought up by the senior minister. The associate minister was female. Although a lot of people wanted to discuss it, the discussion was cut off very abruptly by people who didn't even want to talk about it—which is absolutely *not* the way you get different people to want to stay in a church. You have to have a process which gives everybody a lot of time and opportunity to say what they want to say; to know that people are listening even if they disagree; and that they're going to listen respectfully.

One's conclusion may be, "Well, okay. That's your point of view. I totally disagree with it." But people need to know that their views are going to be listened to. Then one can come away, once the issue has been resolved, and not leave the church. If you go through a process, which is what we do now, you get an issue like whether we should become an open and affirming church. We decide we're not going to decide in six months, and we're not going to decide by the end of the year. We're going to go through a process with educational forums where people are going to speak about the issues. We're going to let people say what they need to say, and then we're going to vote on it. A lot of people just want to get on with it and vote. . . . Without such a process, it comes down to, "Let's shut these people up because it becomes too divisive." I heard the word "divi-sive" used repeatedly, and then we decided that we're just going to discuss difficult issues, do it in the open and at length, that it's not going to be divisive. And, lo and behold, it's not divisive!

MORGAN-WELCH: [Speaking as an African American,] I think it's a critical matter, this idea that people who say painful, even racist things, that it's divisive. It isn't as though people of color don't hear such things in other quarters where there isn't an opportunity for reconciliation. So this is a real opportunity. You keep coming together.

[A continuing problem at Center Church is the one of language. Whereas earlier immigrant groups learned English, dealing with Spanish has been an issue of contention in a number of ways and is not yet resolved. It is one of the issues that is being worked through with the process discussed above. Robin Roy is a longtime European American member of Center Church. Larry Roeming, also European American, is a more recent member.]

ROBIN ROY: We realized what we were talking about was how we could be welcoming to people other than ourselves, and that there were issues of language; there were issues of culture; there were issues of sexual orientation. It is my perception that it really was a sort of multifaceted project to start with. We wanted to be a welcoming and inclusive congregation. When the issue of language came up, people said they were not opposed to other languages as such, but why have Spanish and not have other languages as well?

The deacons said one of their goals is to incorporate into the service of worship more diversity through such means as music. Over time, as we build these things into our liturgical year, people are going to assume that it's part of our worship life together.

LARRY ROEMING: I think the long-range history of Center Church is such that there aren't a lot of people who really have racist attitudes; I mean, because of a certain automatic racism just from being white, sometimes you don't realize you're benefiting from things that aren't laid out for someone else. But any sort of conscious racism I haven't heard. It's because our whole history has been a welcoming one, that the whole language thing was sort of startling to me.

Two Hispanic deacons said about the language debate, "It's such a little thing, why is it causing such a problem?" Which is kind of my attitude, too. There's a story I'm telling second-hand. Two Hispanic deacons made a decision in preparing the altar which was disputed by one of the long-time white New England members. Later one of the Hispanic deacons said to me, "It was almost as if the person wasn't respecting us because of that." I think it's important for the Caucasians in the congregation to understand that people of color are going to notice it in that way.

Is it possible to discuss such things? Also, to find out why it is that some groups always sit together during coffee hours, dinners, etc.

ROEMING: I think most of the members who are involved in the church are willing to discuss this. We've done a lot of things such adult classes and retreats, for example, where that kind of discussion is allowed and encouraged.

ROY: We have an opportunity in our church, which is a small enough group of people, to make something work well—something which is, in a way, representative of the larger society. There've been some interesting things in adult groups, too, and one thing was very eye-opening to me. Around the time of the Christopher Columbus anniversary when we talked about the white man coming to the New World, a Cuban member of our church described what he learned as a child in Cuba and compared it with what we had learned here in New England. He also did a program about the role of Hispanic Americans in United States history, and how—as with black people, as with women, as with a lot of particular groups—their contributions had never been acknowledged in mainstream history.

[In the city of Hartford, with a population of approximately 100,000, European Americans are in the minority, with slightly larger percentages of African Americans and Hispanics, and smaller groups of Vietnamese, Cambodians, Chinese, Koreans, Japanese, and, now, more people from Europe.]

ROEMING: Center Church has a much larger percentage of professional people than the city of Hartford, and the professionals are relatively evenly divided among various racial/ethnic groups in the membership.

What do you do about outreach?

ROY: Most new people at Center Church came because they already knew somebody who was a member, or else they were educated people seeking out something they felt they couldn't find in the suburbs.

ROEMING: There certainly hasn't been an effort not to attract working class people, but that as an issue hasn't been specifically addressed. We know that we need to build our membership, and how to do that has been a struggle. People say that the best way to attract new members is for members to talk to other people. If that's the case, then the proportion of working class to professionals probably wouldn't change. We haven't really made any concerted effort in that direction, although an attempt was made when a previous Spanish-speaking intern made serious efforts to establish connections with the nearby Hispanic neighborhood.

It seems to me that a church is one of the few really safe places for different people to be together and talk about those differences with each other. If Center Church could do that better, and sort of spread the word, my best vision would be that some of that notion would catch on in Hartford and, perhaps, expand.

ROY: I really believe in what the church is trying to do here. It isn't wildly popular. It's not a quick fix, because for generations people have held certain opinions of other groups of people, and what their role was in the world. There's a lot of work to be done so that we may live together more harmoniously.

Our deacons are mixed color, mixed language, and mixed sexual orientation. They're a very critical group in our church because of their call to help support the minister, and of leading the worship life of the church. Everyone is certainly integrated into the leadership of the church.

ROEMING: I think one of the lessons you learn from being at Center Church is not to make assumptions. If that's all you learn, there's some progress made.

[The following comments were made by the Reverend J. Alan McLean, pastor of Center Church, and European American, in a telephone interview.]

I really believe that my role is to be the participant in the process; certainly, to declare the vision from the pulpit; to interpret the biblical truth. If you look at the people Jesus gathered around him, you can't find a more varied, a more diverse group of folks, some of whom were part of the mainstream establishment, and some who clearly weren't. I talk about this a lot, in both formal and informal settings. Formally, I need to interpret this in the way we conduct our worship. I see as one of my key roles, constantly trying to encourage us as a congregation to listen respectfully to one another. I believe that respectful, careful listening is the key to a diverse, pluralistic, multicultural faith community.

When I came, I did start doing some things differently. I'm a consensus person and a team player. I take seriously the leadership of the laity and I brought an immediate style that was different from some of my predecessors. I like to think of myself as not a controlling person, but I am also not without my convictions, which I shall convey. If I were to do this again, I would bring the same sense of "Come, let us reason and work together." It is a style I feel good about. I think people have responded to it, and that it has helped bring us to where are, and where we're trying to go.

Two ceremonies that have become part of our worship life emphasize our diverse heritages. On Worldwide Communion Sunday we have a tradition of bringing breads from various cultures—Chinese, African, Swedish, etc.—which are then used in the service of communion. On Pentecost we use a variety of languages during the service, often in praying the Lord's Prayer.

Dan Romero asks the following questions: How much sameness is necessary for a community to be a community? How much diversity can a community absorb and still maintain community? They are important questions, and, I think, go to the heart of our ministry.

First Baptist Church
Los Angeles, California

The following paragraphs from **First Baptist News,** *May 29, 1995, opened a report to the congregation by Dr. John H. Townsend, Senior Pastor of First Baptist Church, Los Angeles, California.*

Less than one mile from the steps of our church is the corner of Third and Vermont. It is a busy corner, populated constantly by cars and people. *Los Angeles Times* columnist Peter King says that "there is no intersection like it anywhere else in the land." He adds, "On display here is what might be called the real California, or perhaps more accurately, the next

California." That observation relates to the three census tracts that come together at Third and Vermont, each counting about ten thousand people. By countries of origin these people hail from Mexico, Bangladesh, El Salvador, China, Korea, the Philippines, Japan, Thailand, Africa, the United States—and may other places besides.

When you walk along Vermont as I sometimes do, or if you drive that way to reach the Hollywood Freeway, you take as a matter of course the businesses and signboards that line the strip malls and adjacent properties. A sampling of the stores and signs around Third and Vermont introduces us to: The Famous Korean Dumpling House; $1 Chinese Food; Agencia de Viajes; Hons Body Shop; California Donuts; La Ygriega Restaurant; Korean Sushi and Noodle; "Fly to the Mythical Island of Bali"; H.O.T. Thai Seafood; "Von's is Value"; Mecca Hallal Meats; "BankAmericard Has a New Face: Yours." There are two supermarkets, a large drug store, a variety of sidewalk merchants and currently subway construction barriers all converging on Third and Vermont. The Islamic Center of Southern California is close by, as well. It has been said that every possible ingredient in the human stew can be found in that neighborhood, "all tossed together in fairly equal measure."

It is . . . here that First Baptist Church finds its calling as the last decade of the current millennium rushes on. The rapid changes and the complexity of our society call to mind the words of composer John Cage. He said, "I can't understand why people are frightened of new ideas. I'm frightened of the old ones." Our dilemma is in knowing how to respond to both the new and the old, to the radically different and the traditionally same. Ours also is a situation not unlike that in which the first Christians found themselves: we, too, confront a world of radical diversity where many are strangers to the Gospel and reflect traditions markedly different from our own.

Yet God has placed us here. Would that we could be like the men of Issachar, described in the Old Testament Scriptures. Issachar was one of the Twelve Tribes of Israel and at the time David was about to become king, this tribe counted two hundred chiefs, plus any number of rank and file members. Of these chiefs of Issachar it was said, they had an understanding of the time; they knew what Israel ought to do. It is wisdom like this that a church like ours requires in times like these. The sons of Issachar were, as the Bible says, "sound judges of the times who know what Israel should do and the best time to do it." In our city, not unlike a modern-day Tower of Babel, the manner and timeliness of doing things is our constant challenge. . . .

It is here . . . that our congregation is called to witness and to serve. We are in this place to communicate a spiritual humility that says that we are all children of one heavenly parent and are meant to live as brothers and sisters of one another.

Conversation with Ruth S. Morales

Pastor Ruth S. Morales was born in Mexico, but has lived in the United States since she was a small child. After previous careers as an aeronautical engineer and teacher of English as a Second Language, she was ordained as a Baptist clergyperson, and has served as Associate Pastor with the Reverend Dr. John H. Townsend since 1986. The following comments by Pastor Morales were made in a telephone interview, August 1995.

Our membership is just under 775, and our weekly attendance is approximately 300. About sixty percent of our worshipers belong to minority groups. We have 89 Hispanic families that are part of my pastoral responsibility. In earlier years [1960s)]most of the Hispanics in our church were Cuban refugees that our church sponsored. They were mostly professional people who wanted to integrate and start a new life in the United States. Now the new Hispanic population comes from Mexico and Central and South America for both political and economic reasons. Many of them come with no legal papers. They have to work very hard to survive; their lives are very complicated. Most of them were wonderful church leaders in their countries. Their worship style was not as traditional as ours, but that's been good for us. *They* are evangelizing *us*.

I am bilingual [English/Spanish] and very multicultural, and therefore it is easy for me to associate with all minorities. They see me mix in all circles and people feel comfortable with me, Anglos included. So I am definitely seen as associate minister of the whole church and not only the minister for Hispanics. In Dr. Townsend and me they see a team. The only thing I don't do is preach often, and that is partly by choice. Included in our staff are part-time pastors, the Rev. Sam Kim, Korean, and Mr. Kenneth Ho, Filipino.

My philosophy is, "People are people, and we are all God's people." We work very hard in stating we are one family and one church. Our bulletin states that we are ecumenical, interracial, international, and of course affiliated with the American Baptist Churches, U.S.A. All our boards have members from all ethnic groups, and sometimes when we have potential leaders who feel they don't speak the English language very well, I say, "You speak enough. There'll be someone there to help, but we need your leadership qualities." We encourage them and because of that we reinforce the sense that we're one church. The Hispanics are in their twenties to fifties for the most part, and are the ones who volunteer in Sunday School, potlucks, rummage sales, and other all-church activities. They feel comfortable working because they can see they are needed.

The riots in Los Angeles triggered by the Rodney King beating in 1992 occurred on a Wednesday night, and on the following Sunday when we had our worship service, most of the people there were minorities since they lived in the community. Many of the Anglos stayed away, possibly out of fear of the unknown. Most of them moved out many years ago, and their children who are in their forties also moved out. It is a fact that even though they live outside of the community, they are very supportive of the congregation and come from long distances for worship service. They also continue to provide leadership and monetary resources. After the riots, we had to do a lot of reflection—not so much for the effect it had on our congregation (although we did have a Korean person lose his business) but on the whole community. The Hispanics from our church were very embarrassed about Hispanics who were caught up in vandalizing. Even though we know that much of what occurred was just that people got caught up emotionally, there is an underlying thought that many, many people feel they've been ignored and discriminated against. We did a lot of soul-searching, and I believe it strengthened us to know that we need to work harder at making people feel good and important and to help bring about equity, justice, and understanding. The hope, in this church setting, is to create a family—to work hard at being a family. The test of our Christianity is proven if we can put up with each other, accept and love each other the way we are.

The church has done considerable work with young people in the community, for it is our feeling that the church needs to be open and accessible. For instance, we have an arrangement with the YMCA to use our gym. They provide the personnel for a daily program with the neighborhood youth. We also have a daily program for school children who are out of school on the year around school schedule, which is managed by the Girl Scout agency. There is also a tutoring program for youth offered every day with the help of college students from UCLA and Los Angeles State University.

Our Korean membership is a bit more reserved. We are surrounded by large, powerful Korean churches that have affected us by their large numbers. We do have five English-as-a-Second-Language classes and a citizenship class for Koreans.

The African Americans that we have are very active and are good leaders. They're not in large numbers. I don't really know why, but I believe that it is partly because the community is not African American. We work well with the American Baptist churches that are African American. In our Los Angeles City Mission Region, much of the leadership is African American.

We have to keep working at what we are trying to do, "we" meaning the world—the city. It's not easy to break down barriers. The way to break down barriers is really to mix with people, which in turn will break down the fears that people are this or the other. The only way to get to know people is to reach out intentionally and get to know them. We all have a lot of commonalities. I recognize that we need to have churches that are all Spanish or all Korean, but I think the ideal way is to be open and bring in different groups where all have space and freedom to be, and where none will lose what they bring and everybody will be enriched. I believe the way this happens, really, is when the clergy leadership is a team—and lay leadership is allowed to be free. We need to be totally people-oriented and service-oriented. Power comes through service—not through anything else.

The church doesn't belong to one group only. The church belongs to the people, and that needs to be practiced. It's hard and difficult, but you keep on practicing it. And whenever one hears little things that interfere with this goal, you don't bawl people out, but you keep working at it and bring the awareness: "You know, that was not necessary—that statement implies something." We say it in a kind way, because many times things are not said intentionally. It's just the way one is brought up which often brings out our prejudices. We work hard at breaking that. My philosophy is to encourage people and help them feel competent, that they have abilities, that we're all in the same business of serving the Lord, and that in serving the Lord we worship him as we serve each other and help each other.

From the Mission Statement of Oakhurst Presbyterian Church

Oakhurst Presbyterian Church is a community of diversities. We come from different places, from different economic levels, from different countries of the world. We are a church in the city. Our life has known the movement of the city: we were once all of one kind. Then our church became multiracial and felt small and insignificant. And our people were afraid, afraid of ourselves from different races, afraid of ourselves from different cultures. The faithfulness of those who stayed and those who came gave us courage. By God's power we have been given grace through what we thought was our weakness. In the midst of our fears God has empowered us to confront God's truth in the world. In Jesus Christ the dividing walls of hostility have been broken down. Though we are born into diverse earthly families, our life together at Oakhurst has led us to affirm that we are called to be one family through the life, death and resurrection of Jesus Christ. . . .

At Oakhurst the compelling sermons bring meaning to our stories and clarify the connectedness of our lives. The preaching sounds the Call to Justice. The Oakhurst message is not always a comfortable message. Rather, it is that we must seek to do God's will even when in conflict with the demands of the world. Our worship and work confirm that we are not impotent, that we are not just victims within this society, but through the love of Christ we are empowered and are therefore responsible to act. We are The Good News realized. The work of our ministers guides our diverse peoples to weave the fabric that is our tapestry, Oakhurst Presbyterian Church.

From Many Threads, One Tapestry.
From Many Streams, One River.
From Many Branches, One Tree.
We Are Oakhurst.

Inez Fleming

Inez Fleming, an Elder at Oakhurst Presbyterian Church, Decatur, Georgia, gives her church the gift not only of love, but of directness and honesty, as she writes about the difficulties and joys in her life as an African American woman in a multicultural congregation. Ms. Fleming's essay forms a chapter in the book While We Run This Race *by Oakhurst's pastor, Nibs Stroupe, in collaboration with Ms. Fleming. Inez Fleming works closely with Pastor Stroupe in developing and leading workshops that promote multiracial leadership and understanding.*

To make progress for justice, I must engage white folks as well as my people. When I engage white folks, I am told that I am angry and that I should not raise issues of race. When I engage white folks, my people see me as selling out or they attack me for making white people uncomfortable. I have felt this same process at my church, Oakhurst Presbyterian Church. As has been indicated, we are a multiracial church, but we have our share of problems, too. We are not without the dynamics of race. After all, we have a white male pastor, and I have learned that this is usually the case in these kinds of multiracial churches. But, how many whites would come to a church with a black, male pastor? I'm getting ahead of myself here—let me go back a bit.

Until 1986, I attended and worked hard in the traditional black Methodist church. That year I married an African American man who was a member of Oakhurst. I came over to Oakhurst with the intention of winning my husband back over to my church, the black church. I could not believe that any self-respecting African American would be a part of a church with a lot of white folks and especially with a white man as a pastor. The black church was about the only place we could be ourselves.

I discovered that Oakhurst was not quite what I thought it was. Oh, there were white folks there who troubled me, to be sure; but there was also a glimmer of hope. There actually seemed to be some white folks there who genuinely wanted to learn about their own racism and about my people. Motives are never pure, but there seemed to be a willingness to listen to us and to our story. I also heard through my involvement at Oakhurst that I didn't always have to be "nice." I heard that to affirm my identity as an African American was positive. I also heard that it was not only permissible to acknowledge the power of racism in this diverse community of faith—it was an absolute necessity, part of the faith journey.

I began to sense the possibility of a shift in myself, but I was extremely hesitant about getting involved at Oakhurst. It was all new to me—there were white folks there, with a white, male leader. As a black person, all my warning signs went up—proceed with extreme caution. To make yourself vulnerable as a black person to white folks is to put yourself at great risk. I was torn between what I felt was loyalty to my people and an increasing desire to test out this multiracial congregation. In my opinion, you could not put black and white together in any healthy fashion. Yet, Oakhurst did need plenty of help in this area, and I was hearing from the white, male pastor that it could happen with integrity. I could be myself as a black person and not be crushed. So, I decided to try it, amid much protest from my black friends. After all, if I really believed what I had always professed to believe—that *all* persons are brothers and sisters in Christ—then I would need to begin to relate to the white part of the family. Easier said than done!

I felt great frustration at first. I couldn't read the signals of white folks, and I didn't know how to translate them. With the help of the pastor and others, I began to be able to find sources for translation. My biggest concern in becoming involved, however, was not my encounters with white folks at Oakhurst. My biggest concern was how my involvement and views would be received by my people at Oakhurst. The strong position I intended to take as a black person was not part of the picture at Oakhurst at that time. The thoughts I began to share as a black person were not always welcome. Although there were some tense moments because I was raising the issue of race, thanks to God things began to shift and to fall into place.

There are still tremendous problems at Oakhurst related to "race," but I believe that we have made a start that is real. I recognize that in my lifetime "race" will always be present, but my constant prayer is that we all can work toward that time when we all will be seen first as human beings, as a variety of colors in God's garden. I am now an elder at Oakhurst, on its governing board, and the chairperson of the Christian Education Committee. I traveled to Nicaragua in 1993, and I learned that white folks act the same in other countries as they do here. I also learned in Nicaragua of the indomitable human spirit, which refuses to be crushed by any system. I stay involved at Oakhurst because I continue to be filled with joy when I can say without fear or concern of being shunned: "Say it loud! I'm black, and I'm proud!"

I am often asked by my friends and acquaintances, "Why even bother? Why are you over there devoting your time and talents and energy to white folks? Why not invest all of this in your own people?" I must admit that sometimes I ask myself the same questions: Why do I work with white folks? Why do I feel that working with white folks is so important in the struggle against racism? Am I cheating my own people by spending time and energy on white folks? The answer to me is clear—every person has an obligation to actively participate in seeking to create a better world for succeeding generations. The only way this will happen is for all to address the number one problem in our culture—racism. To address racism means to encounter white folks.

I made the difficult and perilous decision to become involved at Oakhurst, to engage the white folks there. It has been a roller-coaster ride, with feelings of accomplishment and feelings of idiocy. I have experienced difficult encounters with white folks and with my people at Oakhurst. As it was in the business world [In Fleming's professional life], so it is with the church. I *expect* difficulties with white folks, but I am disappointed with difficulties with my folks.

I am not certain that any good has come from these encounters, but at least I have learned that the system of race has the power to tear apart my people. Race is a monster, and all of us who are black must face it. Indeed, I prefer the name "black" to "African American" because I take the white folks' negative image of me and stand up to them: "Say it loud—I'm black and proud." To say that "black is beautiful" is not to misunderstand or misuse the language. It is to comprehend it only too well and to challenge it on its own terms. No begging to be recognized as a human being, no seeking to please the white folks. Just to be. And to be proud of that being, whatever white folks may decide to call it.

I have not always been as strong in my sense of blackness. While I was always proud to be black, I also had difficult times in dealing with my blackness. There was a period in my life when I had accepted some of the white definition of being black. I came to believe that if my people had problems, the only reason for the problems was that something was wrong with us and that race had nothing to do with it at all. Even though I knew the power of race, I felt that we should have bettered ourselves, that if we worked hard enough, we would succeed.

I have since learned better. I have relearned the system of race, this time from both an analytical and an experiential perspective. My people and I still have a lot to learn. Many of us have fallen into the trap of materialism. We believe that we can prove our self-worth by the material things we acquire. Many of us believe that if we could just get properly educated and get a good job, we would be accepted by whites. This is a white lie, a devious diversion from the system of race. Although white folk want us to believe this lie, the truth is that white folks do not intend to accept us as human beings and do not intend to share power with us. This truth is a given in the system of race, and it should never be forgotten. Never.

I have encountered these struggles at Oakhurst among my people. When I assert my identity as a black woman at Oakhurst, my own people tell me that I am too negative or that I am antiwhite. Once, a sister introduced me as a black racist to a visitor at the church. A discussion in our church's governing body was particularly difficult for me. I am an elder, which is an elected position, and part of that governing body. The committee that I chair as elder recommended to the governing body, the Session, that we endorse the formation of a black women's group in our church. Nibs and I anticipated trouble on this recommendation, and we tried to prepare for it. But, we were not prepared for it; indeed, I don't know that I could ever have been prepared for it.

The problem that we encountered on this question at Oakhurst was our own self-image. We are a multiracial church, and part of our image as Oakhurst is a wonderful community where everyone gets along. The reality is something different, however. Please don't misunderstand me. Oakhurst is a significant and powerful community of faith because it has dared to try to tell and to live the truth that the Gospel is more important than race. It is a place unlike most places in this society. If I did not think that it was significant and that it offered possibilities, I would not be at Oakhurst.

Like all approaches to race, however, we at Oakhurst, too, want to move quickly over race without really encountering it, "we" meaning both black and white. So, when the recommendation was made to start a black women's group in a place that was supposed to be beyond race, it struck a lot of hearts. One sister made a strong point: If a white woman had come with a recommendation to start a white women's group,, we would turn it down without discussion. So, why should we promote a group that seems to oppose what Oakhurst believes? A brother made the point that we were emphasizing race too much at Oakhurst and that this recommendation was evidence of that. One white woman commented that while she could see a need for such a group, an endorsement by us would be the same as endorsing the system of race.

Another sister supported the recommendation, saying that she felt the need for this group. She felt that many black women at Oakhurst faced immense problems from their own particular histories and from the culture at large, and that they needed a place to share them and to seek solutions. She also said that we were not being realistic if we felt that the group would be the same if white women came. The sharing would simply not be the same because black women were not accustomed to sharing their lives with white folks; to do so was to invite destruction.

During this discussion, Nibs, my pastor and friend, disappointed me. He moderated the meeting; and while he gave verbal support to the proposal, I noticed a shift in the discussion as he led us through it. I don't know whether it was caused by his whiteness or his desire to avoid a split in the governing body, since the discussion indicated a close vote. He began to steer us toward a compromise in which the Session would allow the group to meet in our building but would not formally endorse it. Most of the elders seemed agreeable to this until it came to me. I would not accept it. At this point, Nibs became conscious of what he had done; and I do appreciate that he then publicly stated that with his input he had steered us away from the original motion and toward the compromise. He apologized. White people never cease to amaze me!

The motion to endorse a black women's group was back before us. Then the real turning point came; for me it was both good news and bad news. A white sister spoke in support of the proposal, saying that she understood the objections and the seeming contradiction but felt that we ought to listen to the reality. The real question was not how it would appear but whether we wanted to assist black women in our congregation. If we wanted to help them deal with the power of race that sought to crush their lives both individually and communally, then we ought to try to respond in this manner. From my point of view, her comments were crucial because of the timing and because she was white. The motion passed by a close vote of 5–4. The vote crossed racial lines—three blacks and two whites for it and two blacks and two whites against it. One brother abstained, and the pastor didn't vote.

Why did I say the white sister's comments were both good news and bad news? Why have I gone into such detail about this decision? The reason is that this discussion is central to my struggles as a black woman in engaging the system of race and because it tells so much about what is really going on. My white sister's comments were good news because it was clear that she was listening and that she was understanding. It can happen—white people can hear us and listen to us. I know that her own personal history had helped her develop sensitivity, but I also like to think that her being a part of Oakhurst helped to develop her sensitivity. She even called me later to tell me that she appreciated my persistence and that she had some sense of the difficulty of the process for me. And it was good news because I do believe that her comments came at a crucial time.

It was bad news to me because the crucial comments came from a white person. I am not saying that the earlier comments by the sister in favor of the proposal were not crucial. They were crucial because it affirmed that it was not just "bad" Inez's proposal. Yet, I cannot help but feel that the favorable comments from a white person tipped the scale in favor of the motion.

This decision was important to me because, although it went the way I felt it should go, it has reinforced my sense that in multiracial settings such as Oakhurst, my sisters and brothers get uncomfortable when someone like me comes along to raise issues of race. It is as if we are still in the mode of making white people feel comfortable, just as we've always been. If the white pastor raises the issue, that is irritating but acceptable because he is white and the pastor. If a black sister raises the issue, she must be punished for getting out of her place and making both whites and blacks uncomfortable. In an all-black church, this recommendation about a black women's group would need no discussion. And people wonder why some of us tend toward "separatism"!

What does it mean to be black? It means to be in the storm—to be constantly criticized for rocking the boat. It is painful and angering and frustrating. I have many unanswered question: Should I spend so much time with white folks, trying to get them to understand black folks, trying to get them to understand the power of racism? Is it right to take my energy and use it in what I feel is sometimes an impossible mission? Am I cheating my own people by not giving them one hundred percent? These and many other questions haunt me as I encounter the system of race. Perhaps what haunts me the most, however, is that I don't know if I'll ever find the answers. Yet, I know I must try. And, I have crossed the line now. Here I am at Oakhurst.

David Ng

In these extracts from a longer essay, "Sojourners Bearing Gifts," David Ng addresses the need of Asian Americans for a Christian education that does not deny them, as people of God, their natural identity as people of a particular ethnic background; that being a Christian does not require being one "in imitation of white, Anglo-Saxon, Protestant standards." Dr. Ng is Professor of Christian Education at San Francisco Theological Seminary, San Anselmo, California.

There is not yet a widely accepted term for the peoples and cultures I include in the phrase, "Pacific Asian Americans." This broad phrase includes many nationalities, ethnic groups, cultures, and histories, ranging from Samoan to Hawaiian (of Hawaiian or Asian ancestry) to Filipino to Indonesian to Malaysian to Cambodian to Vietnamese to Chinese to Korean to Japanese to any number of other groups who share broad commonalities of geography and some commonalities of racial and historical background. In every case I am referring to these peoples in their American or Canadian environment. These persons are immigrants and their children. With their Pacific or Asian background they remain "hyphenated Americans or Canadians," marginalized by physical characteristics as well as national origin.

My own Chinese American background provides the basis for much of the material in this presentation. This particularity provides focus for the material but it can be granted that much of the material has application to other Pacific Asian American situations as well. . . .

The large wave of Chinese who migrated to America over a hundred years ago were seeking "Gum San," the "Golden Mountain." Political turmoil in China, economic upheaval, natural disaster, social dislocation, and similar impoverishing forces pushed the Chinese out of China. The intrusion of Western commercial, national, and religious expansion with its lure of economic and educational opportunity pulled the Chinese to the shores of California, the land of Gum San. The fascinating details are well accounted elsewhere, particularly by writers who have freed themselves from the narrow bounds of an American assimilationist mentality.[1] What is relevant here is that the early Chinese immigrants came to the western hemisphere to seek their fortunes and then to return to their homeland. This migrant group had little interest in adopting western ways or in being assimilated into western culture. A few Christian missions and religious education classes were established. They were significant not in number but in serving as a voice of advocacy for the immigrant Chinese. However, these Chinese churches saw as their major task that of taking the Christian message to China.

Going back to China proved difficult for many Chinese and became virtually impossible during World War II. The Chinese reluctantly concluded that they were in the United States and Canada to stay. Their children knew no other country but the United States or Canada. The Chinese began to buy into the American Dream and made efforts to meld into the melting pot of American democracy. Short of dyeing their hair blond or straightening their eye shapes, many Chinese made great efforts to play down their Asian characteristics and to fit into an American mode of life.

Another turning point in the Chinese American experience occurred in 1965.[2] Twenty years after the world war in which Americans and Chinese fought side by side, and nearly a hundred years after oppressive laws were first passed against the "heathen Chinee," the immigration laws were broadened to enable many more Chinese to emigrate to the United States. At one point the Chinese came at the rate of a thousand each month. Increased numbers along with the development of Chinese American second and third generation young adults as social activists on behalf of their own people, led to significant changes in Chinese American self perceptions. A more intentional and informed sense of Chinese American identity developed. Self-determination became a political issue and there were many sophisticated demands for fair treatment for Chinese Americans and other Asian Americans in all dimensions of North American life. Power in Chinese American communities shifted from groups protecting the status quo to younger groups seeking equality and fair economic and political treatment. Young persons were leading by serving as community workers. Pan-Asian American coalitions formed to advocate for justice. Along with other ethnic groups, Pacific Asian Americans (and Canadians in their situation) have rejected the old melting pot myth and have helped to establish a new myth of a mosaic of American cultures which in its pluralism accepts great cultural diversity.

The Chinese American churches—few in number and a minority factor even in Chinese American communities—reflect the history of the Chinese Americans in general. At first Chinese American churches looked to China for leadership and for mission purpose. Later the churches provided pastoral care for the Chinese who found they would be staying, probably permanently, in America. While espousing a western faith the churches provided Chinese social, language, and ethical expressions. Some Chinese Americans found assimilation in the suburbs and in predominantly Caucasian churches; the majority of Chinese Americans maintained certain traditional ways by staying in Chinese churches, even a the expense of driving many miles to return to the home church. Even after the changes of the 1960's and 1970's the Chinese American churches provided a buffer from the assimilative forces at work. These churches, with one or two exceptions,[3] looked to Hong Kong for leadership in preaching and teaching, and maintained as a major thrust a ministry to persons who were immigrants. Even where second and third generation Chinese Americans were predominant in number and financial strength, they were not in total control of the programmatic priorities or political structures of the churches.

Ministry with the foreign-born remains a major priority today, but Chinese American churches now reflect current trends such as the use of study materials in English, growing leadership by second and third, even fourth generation Chinese Americans, and positive or even aggressive attitudes towards ethnic identification. . . .

Pacific Asian American churches need a Christian education which authenticates their ethnic identity. If this is not the major issue in education it is certainly a strong example of a major need. When Pacific Asian Americans are called into membership in the community of faith, the church, they gain an identity as the People of God. This identity does not require them to deny their natural identity as persons of a particular ethnic background. Nor are Pacific Asian Americans required to become white Americans, or "white, Anglo-Saxon Protestants" in order to be People of God. The liberating, life-giving, identifying message of the Bible is that becoming the People of God fulfills one's full human identity. As it states in Galatians, "There is neither Jew nor Greek, there is neither slave nor free, there is neither male nor female; for you are all one in Christ Jesus. And if you are Christ's you are Abraham's offspring, heirs according to the promise." (Gal. 3:28-29) Admittedly many in the past have interpreted this passage to mean that everyone assumes a Christian identity, and identification as a Jew or Greek, male or female, etc., is rendered immaterial. Pacific Asian Americans themselves have been the ones who have given the church a fresh interpretation of this passage, or at least have recalled the church to a neglected understanding that when one is in Christ and is a part of Christ's community, one is accepted fully and is freed to be one's own, full self. A Greek can be a Greek, and Jew can be a Jew; a Japanese American can be a Japanese American, a Samoan can be a Samoan—no one has to deny one's own personality, integrity, or heritage. All are accepted as they are. One's identity is authenticated and accepted.

For too long in America people had to be Christians in an "American way." Pacific Asian Americans had to be Christian in imitation of white, Anglo-Saxon, Protestant standards. This narrow-minded version of the gospel is now rejected and the church must proclaim the more inclusive gospel which invites and accepts all people including women, ethnic minority persons, racial minority persons, and persons with handicapping conditions.

The process of discovering an inclusive gospel has been painful. A quick comparison of certain characteristics in Anglo American culture and in Korean culture can exemplify the pain minority persons have had to endure. In an article entitled "Cultural Influences on the Education of Korean-American Children," Young Pai, a professor at the University of Missouri at Kansas City, makes these comparisons:[4]

1. In Anglo American culture persons hold individual rights in high regard. They exercise individual rights, self-expression, and self-assertiveness. Personal identity is defined by personal achievement, often accomplished in a competitive atmosphere.

    In Korean culture, reflected in Korean American culture, persons are held in high regard when they perform their duties and responsibilities to the groups to which they belong, and conform to the group's expectations. Personal identity is defined in relation to one's group.

2. In Anglo American culture all persons are viewed as equals. Interpersonal relationships are informal and communication across various lines are encouraged, such as between parents and children.

    In Korean American culture individuals belong someplace within a hierarchy of relationships and follow elaborate rules regarding social behavior and communication. Children defer to adults.

3. In Anglo American culture individuals, as equals, participate in democratic processes of decision making. Teaching, learning, and decision-making structures are loosely structured; teachers and parents often relate to children as friends and counselors.

    In Korean American culture individuals in a hierarchical structure obey their superiors and accept their teaching and directions.

4. In Anglo American culture analytical and objective thinking is emphasized and factual information is separated from personal feeling.

    In Korean American culture subjective and objective thinking often are intermingled. A person's deeds are judged in association with the person herself or himself.

This comparison, using Korean American characteristics, exemplifies Pacific Asian American personal and interpersonal characteristics. It is not hard to imagine that persons whose culture values a different set of personal expressions, communications, and thinking styles would find it oppressive to live by another set of values and styles—styles not necessarily better than their own. So it is a happy and liberating discovery to find out, through the good news of the Christian gospel, that one does not have to be western and white to be a Christian. Nor does one have to be eastern—after all, Pacific Asian Americans are not either/or types of persons, but live in an in-between state which is both/and; they are Pacific Asian, and they are also American.

The positive affirmation of ethnic identity then is a major educational task for the entire church. This must be accepted and practiced by both Pacific Asian Americans and by ethnic majority Americans. The recovery of the inclusiveness of the gospel, a message which has lain fallow in the Bible for centuries, provides the warrant for this affirmation of diversity. The biblical story provides many other warrants and examples, not the least of which is the Cross. Ethnic minority persons such as Pacific Asian Americans can identify with the people of God and with Jesus Christ, because they too know what it is to suffer. The Bible story is their story,

Endnotes

1. Chinese American church historian Wesley S. Woo states that "in recent years there has emerged a growing body of literature detailing the history of Asian and Pacific Islanders in America." Wesley S. Woo, "Exploring Present and Future Dimensions of Multicultural Christian Education: Asian American Perspectives" (Division of Educaction and Ministry, National Council of the Churches of Christ, 1982) p. 1.
2. *Ibid.*, p. 4
3. A significant exception is the Presbyterian Church in Chinatown, San Francisco, and its community center. Donaldina Cameron House, where a comprehensive Christian education program is offered to Chinese American youth. Until recently the program did not deal with Chinese culture or consciously present American

culture, but challenged its members to be critics of all cultures and to be Christian witnesses within a culture.

4. Young Pai, "Cultural Influences on the Education of Korean-American Children," *Footprints* (Summer) 1983, vol. VI, no. 2, pp. 17–19.

too. Not only do minority peoples find comfort in identifying with Jesus' suffering, they can become mediators of this message to the majority in the church. The majority has not had to endure much personal or corporate suffering. The Cross may be an abstraction to them. An ethnic identity which has had to be forged on the anvil of pain can become redemptive suffering not only for one's own identity's sake, but for the sake of the whole church. When Pacific Asian Americans shape their identities they become a gift to the rest of the church.

Joyce Carlson

Joyce Carlson's own mixed cultural roots have made her profoundly aware of the need to affirm the values of more than one tradition. In the following essay she suggests that different or conflicting ways of using language—in the telling of stories, for example—can hamper effective crosscultural communication, and need to be understood. Ms. Carlson is editor of Dancing Sun, an intergenerational crosscultural resource published by the United Church of Canada. She also serves as editor for the First Nations Ecumenical Liturgical Resources Board.

A Place of Coming Together

I grew up on in a multicultural community in the heart of the North American continent near a city called *Winnipeg* by its original Cree inhabitants, meaning *place where the waters come together*, in the Province of *Manitoba*, a derivative of *Manitou-bah* meaning *voice of the Great Spirit*.

This place of waters coming together is a place of cultures coming together. Rich in wildlife and a key to transportation by canoe, the area has been important to the First Nations for centuries. It was the center of the Fur Trade era which lasted a hundred years. By the late 1800s, the balance of nature which First Nations had guarded for generations was upset. Buffalo herds and game upon which they had depended for survival were gone. The people were on the verge of starvation and Canada was interested in expansion.

The Canadian Government respected neither First Nations people nor descendants of the men who served the fur trade and their First nations wives. These mixed-race peoples lived in the land with a mixture of farming skills of European and French Canadian ancestry and an intimate knowledge of the country, hunting, fishing and trapping, of mothers and grandmothers. Rebellions over land were suppressed; leaders were jailed and hanged. Europeans flooded in, attracted by free land and new opportunity.

The pattern of displacement of First Nations peoples is most clear where the expanding eastern and colonial forces are more recent. Confederation occurred three generations ago, at the time my grandparents were born. They represent the different cultures in the area.

A Legacy of Conflict:

One of my earliest memories is an endless nightmare in which my parents were trying to drown each other. I was perched beside the deep waters begging them to stop. They were so involved in their fight they didn't hear me. Neither gave up and neither gave in. The dream didn't ever resolve itself.

Conflict marked our relationships with each other, with grandparents, with community and with the outside world. The conflict would not have been visible outside the family because of a fierce pride. It was important to maintain a strong public face. I hated the conflict.

After years of cross-cultural communication I begin to comprehend the terrifying forces of my earliest memories. When cultures meet, some of the values of some of the cultures are favoured more than others in formal structures of government, church and education. What happened in the cultural mix in this area is that First Nations spiritual understandings, values and languages were not valued. The resulting devastation in First Nations communities is well documented. Mixed-race people often aligned themselves with the white community to give their children the benefits of education and opportunities. Non-English speaking immigrants were next in the pecking order. Those most favoured were English speaking; their world view became the norm.

I knew all my grandparents. One side of the family built the forts; the other was "barricaded" out. A family album with the lineage of my father's family is preserved. My mother's family never referred to that ancestry. When people asked whether she was part "Indian" because of her appearance, she honestly didn't know. She was discouraged from getting a "tan." In my childhood, I was drawn to the laughter, music and dance of her family, but I didn't understand those values to be rooted in the mixed race community. In the midst of all the conflict, I sought escape in the *natural world* and in *literature*. I left home as soon as I could.

A few years later I lived in England. I wept when I saw daffodils bursting through the earth in spring. I loved poetry, had memorized Wordsworth's "Daffodils" by heart as a child. I suddenly understood how he must have felt. The poetry and stories I had learned in my childhood were British. Literature is profoundly contextual. Where then was the literature that would have related to my experience?

I have travelled to ancestral homes in the northern islands of Scotland, northern Sweden, and England. I have never travelled in my own country to the places or tribes of the early First Nations women. *None of them were ever named* in any official archive or record. The only identification beside the names of the male ancestors was: Indian wife. I've now begun to glimpse some of what was lost along with the names.

The Sharing of Story

Two years ago I travelled to a small First Nation community north of my childhood home. As we travelled, an Elder told stories of the country, of the land, the animals, and the trickster Wisahkechak. When we gathered with his community I felt a lightness, a ripple of recognition when "trickster" was mentioned. . . .

Later, I walked with the Elder on the ice of the lake I'd known so well as a child and he explained patterns of ice formation. In the distance I felt I could see the place where the wide, bright sky touched the earth. I felt blessed to have such an intimate glimpse into his world. As I looked back at the shoreline, I saw my own world with new eyes. Trickster was slipping in and out between the trees. I saw why the moose had a loose coat, why weasel had a black tip on his tail. I learned why rabbit had a tuft of fat on the back of his neck. I saw the wonderful way the habits of animals were described. Here was the literature of the country!

I had never heard these stories although they existed all around me. The reason was directly related to the conflict and negation of First Nations culture. The people who held the stories in my family were so inflicted with self hate that they never shared them with their own children and grandchildren.

A friend once asked: "Why do you persist in living like an exile in your own country?" "Excellent question," I snapped, "but I don't know the answer." I now believe a part of the answer is because the conflict of my parents existed *between* them, but *within* me. I didn't belong in either world. I couldn't choose one or another without negating a part of myself. When in the midst of the conflict I turned to the natural world and to literature, I encountered another dimension of the same historic conflict; the literature I loved didn't relate to my experience. This lack of connection increased my alienation.

The depth of the conflict became clear to me when exploring ways to publish oral stories. Elders said that the meaning of stories and prayers in their own languages didn't translate easily, didn't "fit" in the English language. I didn't actually grasp that truth until I began to transcribe oral stories. I then understood that the difference in world view was evident in the *form and structure of stories, as well as content.*

Storytelling is an art form. Oral stories lend themselves to being written in a poetic form. Working from the inside of stories, it was clear that the European style with beginning, middle and endings was related to different thought patterns, reflecting different understandings of life, community and relationships. When we use the same words, we pattern them in different ways, use different underlying structures and have different assumptions about meaning.

These differences in world view have been enormously painful within First Nations communities, especially for children taken from homes to be taught in residential schools. Unfamiliar with the content of courses based on the European culture of their teachers, some felt there was something wrong with themselves when they tried to write and had difficulty expressing themselves. Many understood that the world view reflected in their schoolbooks was different from that of their communities. Those who persisted in maintaining identity and language did so at the risk of severe punishment.

First Nations communities are now developing curricula in schools to reflect their world views. In Canada, there have been apologies to First Nations people by the major churches and a move to self-determination within those denominations.

Where Is the Voice of the Great Spirit Now?

There is a good will in trying to come to terms with cultural differences, but we need to pay close attention to the values and assumptions which have shaped the way our churches function. Language which informs liturgy and worship is rooted in historic structures which may not encourage expressions of other cultures.

I find the differences in world view reflected in content, structure and form of stories to be liberating. My childhood conflict is more understand-able. There were many losers and few winners in the coming together of cultures because some were valued more than others. In not affirming First Nations cultures we all lost a connection to the land and rich tradi-tions. For some of us, it also meant alienation from ourselves. In an in-creasingly multicultural society, this struggle *between* cultures and *within* people will be much more common unless we work intentionally to find ways of "being" together that transcend institutional and language struc-tures which may cause separations between us and within us.

Faith can bring us to unity. I worship in the Anglican Church of Canada, a church with colonial roots. It is patriarchal and hierarchical. Yet it is my community. In my small parish, we struggle with inclusive language and forms of worship which are welcoming of all. One of the ways we work at this is through nurturing community where we are able to share our own stories, where we are free to express our gifts. We are rooted in the present, yet reaching for the new. We must somehow be working at it.

Our churches have a role in bringing healing to the larger society through affirming and respecting differing understandings. Through story, we meet as human beings, we come to greater fullness and are enriched by the variety of experience and expressions of faith. I somehow feel that the voice of the Great Spirit is not a single voice overwhelming and still-ing all others but a voice welcoming and drawing together the many. We need to find ways to expand our understandings so that the *voice of the Great Spirit* may bring healing and reconciliation in an increasingly multicultural society.

POSTSCRIPT

First, we must listen. We must listen to those whom we seek to understand. In a multicultural society, this means that people of each group must learn to understand something of what shapes and motivates, disturbs and delights those from other groups. In a society dominated by one culture, it means people from that culture must grapple with the issues and realities of those from other cultures.

All of us need a voice. *All* of us need to be heard. Indeed, one of the stresses in the current multicultural debate is that people from every group in the society *demand* to be heard. Historically, this has not been popular with the dominant culture. However, for Christians who believe in the shared life of the people of God, it is exactly right. As representatives of the many, various people of God, we must connect and make room for one another, or our "beautiful mosaic" here in the United States and Canada may splinter—and the shards will damage us all.

After we have listened we need to talk. Because listening is the beginning of dialogue. And genuine dialogue can bring deeper understanding. Let us talk with one another. Let us be faithful and clear. And let what we have learned determine what we do and say in our homes, our communities, our public lives, our churches. This is how all of us as members of the human family, God's family, can be a source of healing for today and the future.